PHILOSOPHICAL PSYCHOLOGY

PHILOSOPHICAL PSYCHOLOGY

A New Frontier in Education and Therapy:
Psychological Humanism – Maslow Revisited

William F. O'Neill, PhD
Professor Emeritus, Educational Philosophy
Chair, Department of Social and Philosophical Foundations of Education
University of Southern California

George D. Demos, PhD
Clinical Psychologist Professor Emeritus, Counseling Psychology
California State University, Long Beach

iUniverse, Inc.
Bloomington

Philosophical Psychology
A New Frontier in Education and Therapy:
Psychological Humanism-Maslow Revisited

iUniverse books may be ordered through booksellers or by contacting:

iUniverse
1663 Liberty Drive
Bloomington, IN 47403
www.iuniverse.com
1-800-Authors (1-800-288-4677)

Because of the dynamic nature of the Internet, any web addresses or links contained in this book may have changed since publication and may no longer be valid. The views expressed in this work are solely those of the author and do not necessarily reflect the views of the publisher, and the publisher hereby disclaims any responsibility for them.

Any people depicted in stock imagery provided by Thinkstock are models, and such images are being used for illustrative purposes only.

Certain stock imagery © Thinkstock.

ISBN: 978-1-4759-1611-9 (sc)
ISBN: 978-1-4759-1613-3 (hc)
ISBN: 978-1-4759-1612-6 (e)

Printed in the United States of America

iUniverse rev. date: 9/14/2012

The authors take this opportunity to express their gratitude to those who have been instrumental in the completion of this book.

Special appreciation goes to Dr. John Mize, PhD for his careful and conscientious review of the manuscript and his insightful suggestions.

Additional thanks are given to Dale Anne O'Neill for her persistence, devotion, and day to day guidance that brought this book to fruition.

PREFACE

⎯⎯⎯⎯⎯⎯

This work contains many provocative and profound ideas, some of which may be sensed as offensive by those with rather thin intellectual skins. Some readers in capitalistic societies may take offense at any suggestion that Marx had some good insights about a healthier way to achieve self-actualization than the "work, produce, consume, work, produce, consume, etc." characterization of capitalism made by Jack Kerouac. Some may find it bizarre to read that perhaps Hitler and Stalin were in some ways happier and more self-actualized in their roles as brutal tyrants than they would have been in more "normal" roles.

The range of ideas and thinkers included in this work is extensive, as a brief examination of the references will reveal. Although the references are in some cases incomplete, lacking the edition used, or the publisher, any interested reader will have no difficulty in finding a needed source. Unfortunately, it would be nearly impossible for the authors to provide the complete references at this time. We hope that the kindly reader will pardon this inconvenience.

Although the work lacks an introductory chapter in which a major theme is described, perhaps it will suffice to indicate that the chapters build toward a better understanding of the concepts of self-actualization and peak experience. Essential ideas are examined, such as pain, pleasure, society, ethics, and love, culminating in the concept of peak experience. The insights offered in this work make it worthwhile reading, even though it is not as finely polished as one might wish. Dare to look past the few blemishes in order to see the valuable insights within.

John Mize Ph.D.
Professor of Philosophy (retired)

Table of Contents

1. Subception I

From the empirical-behaviorist point of view, perception is a cognitive encounter that is normally directed by a prior (and frequently sublimated) pre-perceptual autonomic response to the situation-at-hand. Since most discussions of such responses have centered on how they function to mediate repression (and generally on the repression of interiorized personal experiences associated with prior behaviors), it is perhaps easiest to discuss what might be called pre-perceptual sign-learning by discussing how it controls repressed experience in which the individual avoids certain perceptions/meanings by actively directing his consciousness away from them.

In what is probably the most eloquent discussion of symbolism and related topics since Whitehead, philosopher Susanne Langer distinguishes between "signs," which imply three essential terms--subject, sign, and object--and "symbols" which imply four essential terms--subject, symbol, conception, and object (Langer 1957:61). **Signs**, states Langer, are "something to act on". **Symbols**, on the other hand, are "vehicles for the conception of objects". Signs, like the word "smoke," indicate the presence of something. If this something has been previously encountered, it may be interpreted to point to objects or events that are not immediately present but merely implied on the basis of such experience--such as the presence of fire. Signs may lead to elaborate sequences of symbolic extrapolation-- "The smoke is coming from the direction of my house, so perhaps my house is on fire," and so on.

Where Langer is wrong is in holding that "signification" does not figure in symbolization at all" (Langer 1957:64). The fact is that any sign that is recognized on the basis of previous experience to indicate the presence of something else elicits both a memory of the individual's previous encounter with such a sign (with therefore a perception of its status in one's present experience) and, at the same time, a recollection (which is a sort of re-experience) of the emotional impact of such an encounter or encounters. Indeed in a field of competing stimuli--which is the normal situation in the case of virtually all perception/cognition--what occurs can be outlined approximately as follows:

The subject scanned the field autonomically--reacting motor-emotionally to available signs on the basis of their affective intensity in relationship to his prior experience with such signs.

Other things being equal, individuals select stimuli on the basis of their intrinsic emotional (hedonic) valence; they respond to those things which elicit the greatest preperceptual emotional response and then proceed to symbolize (perceive) the situation by progressively reducing the emotional cues (signs) in order of intensity while, at the same time, reconfiguring them in relationship to each other and arriving at some sort of general interpretation.

In other words, viewed developmentally, we are presented with the following sequence of events:

Situationality (the active organism in response to the environment over time)
    (gives rise to)
behavior
    (which produces)

emotional (approach/avoidance) sign-learning
(which evolves into)
sign-identification (labeling), replete with emotionally resonant images
(which gives rise to)
symbolization, which is a sort of generalized labeling
(which ultimately yields both)
Weltanschauung and Selbstauschauung.

Viewed in a more narrow, situational sense, the sequence is essentially as follows:

Encounter--the individual's contemporary motivation in conjunction with the emotional content of the situation (the affective significance of the situation as determined by prior personal experience)

Motor behavior
Emotional responses--electro-chemical autonomic reactions elicited by the behavior and filtered through motor-muscular responses
Perception (situation-specific meaning)
Cognitive responses--generalized meanings (if any) in which the perceptual responses are reprogrammed
Subsequent encounters, and so on, in a circular process.

One of Langer's very significant contributions to epistemology is her discussion of music as a "purely connotational semantic" (Langer 1957:93). The "connotation of a word," she notes, "is the conception it conveys" (Langer 1957:64). "Because the connotation remains with the symbol when the object of its denotation [the actual object to which it refers] is neither present nor looked for, we are able to **think about** the object without reacting to it overtly at all" (Langer 1957:64). Music, she states, is not merely "a language of feeling" (Langer 1957:88).

From the empirical-behaviorist point of view, Langer's approach, viewed in its full expression, is both fascinating and profound. Unfortunately, it is also wrong. Music is a "language of feeling" with which the notes cannot, and, indeed, the entire language of musical notation gives rise to sounds that constitute signs that, in turn, elicit affective responses on the basis of the subject's general familiarity with the affective vocabulary of tones and the other dynamics implicit within music itself. In other words, sound is a constant and continuous dimension of reality itself. Sounds and relationships between sounds are isomorphic with categories of human experience based on constancies within behavior and the realities that underlie such behavior. These sounds have been generalized as the fundamental semantic of music, and music, once formulated, has reinforced and elaborated upon this primal dynamic to create a secondary semantic of its own that employs variations within the same tones, tempos, and rhythms that have evolved out of man's primal responses to everything from his own heartbeat to the sounds of the wind and the waves.

What makes music so potent is that it is universal in a way that symbolic communication can never be. It goes directly to the visceral--the motor-emotional substratum of pre-perceptual (subceptual) responsiveness that mediates all conscious awareness and, at the same time, defies effective translation into discursive symbols.

Repression Revisited
From the empirical-behaviorist's point of view, repression can occur in two ways: (1) by means of perceptually-cued anticipatory-responses, or (2) by means of subception.

Repression by Perceptual Anticipation
Repression may occur in response to perceived (conscious) cognitive cues. In such cases, perception is modified in response to associated cues which occur slightly before the threatening event itself and which therefore make appropriate avoidance-tactics possible. According to Dollard and Miller, one way in which punishment functions is by attaching fear to the cues involved in performing punished responses (Dollard and Miller 1950). In such cases the response of stopping thinking tends to become anticipatory

like any other strongly reinforced response. The individual tends to stop thinking, or to veer off onto a different line of thought, before he reaches the memory of the traumatic incident.

Since stronger fears generalize more widely and perhaps also are transferred farther by higher-ordered conditioning, they stop a wider range of cue-producing responses. In the case of combat veterans, the milder cases lose a relatively few memories directly related to combat; the fairly extreme cases lose a large number of memories; and in the most extreme cases, all responses of thought, perception, and speech are stopped so that the patient is in a complete stupor.

This concept of repression has received particular attention in the writings of psychotherapist Thomas Stampfl who makes it the basis for his entire theory of neurosis. In his book **The Modes and Morals of Psychotherapy**, psychiatrist Perry London summarizes Stampfl's point of view as follows:

"Neurotic behavior is the learned avoidance of conditioned anxiety-provoking stimuli. Conditioned anxiety responses do not occur singly, but in a context where a whole series of hitherto innocent cues become connected with a single traumatic experience. As the avoidance behavior is learned, the organism becomes increasingly sensitized to many cues that were originally quite remote from the source of fear and unrelated to it; eventually some of these cues seem sufficiently frightening to produce avoidance, and the organism runs from them as if they were the true source of anxiety rather than innocent features of the context in which it first occurred. Since, in the ordinary course of events, conditioned stimuli always occur slightly earlier than the events to which they become related, neurotic anxiety is generally learned to a whole series of events, starting with the one that happens closest to the true trauma, whether in time, space, or degree of similarity, and working its way backwards to the elements that are furthest removed from it in the same context. Eventually, the avoidance responses are made to the more remote events even in the complete absence of the ones closer and more relevant to the initial source of fear" (London).

That the emotional spread of effect does in fact lead to a generalization of anxiety from the original fearful situation to psychologically-related objects and events has been substantiated experimentally. As Dollard and Miller indicate:

"... fear can get attached to words if spoken out loud. Experimental evidence indicates that fear attached to a word spoken out loud will generalize to the thought of that word.

"... we would expect the fears that are attached to saying forbidden words and announcing the intent to perform forbidden acts to generalize through thinking these words and thinking about performing these acts. These generalized fears would be expected to be somewhat weaker than the original ones. With enough experience of being punished for the words and acts but not for the thoughts, a discrimination should be learned and further weaken the fears attached to the thought. But if the fears are so strong that the thoughts are repressed, the thoughts will not occur so the fears attached to them cannot be extinguished and no discrimination can be learned" (Dollard and Miller 1950).

Repression by Subception

Repression occurs through subception whenever avoidance is cued by a preconscious autonomic response which serves to divert behavior (and therefore distract attention) away from an anticipated punishment. In this sense, subceptual behavior is cued pre-perceptually on a purely emotional basis. The repression consists, not of a tendency to perform a specific substitute-response, but of a tendency to avoid attending to those things which are experienced motor-emotionally as potentially threatening. As Dollard and Miller indicate:

"After effective punishment, the person tends to feel afraid whenever he thinks about or starts to perform the punished act. This fear tends to motivate stopping, at least in experienced people, and since the stopping or withdrawing eliminates the cues eliciting the fear, it is reinforced by a reduction in the strength of that fear. Thus a child who has been punished for a forbidden act tends to be frightened when he starts to do it and less frightened when he stops. If he stops, the reduction in fear reinforces stopping" (Dollard and Miller 1950).

The tendency to be more perceptually "available" to certain experiences than to others seems to extend, as Berelson indicates, literally to the pupil of the eye. "When looking at interesting or pleasant materials, as compared to neutral ones, the pupil dilates measurably. Conversely, looking at distasteful or disliked materials produces contraction" (Berelson). It has also been found that experimental subjects who have been reinforced to electric shock when exposed to one or the other figure in a reversible figure-ground pattern, are far more likely to perceive the nonshocked figure rather than the shocked one when the pattern is reexposed. In one series of experiments using the "Blackie Pictures," a projective test involving a series of pictures in which a small dog ("Blackie") who is involved in a series of situations fraught with various types of sexual symbolism, it was found that, when the pictures were presented by tachistoscope at a speed approaching that of the average threshold of perception, the subjects took significantly longer in identifying the threatening scenes than in identifying those of a neutral nature. It was also found that the threatening scenes had far greater measurable emotional impact even when presented at exposure times far below the perceptual threshold.

Characteristics of Repressed Behavior

All repressions, whether subceptually-cued or perceptually-cued, share certain common features.

1) They are avoidance-responses which function as a perceptual defense against some real or imaged threat.

2) They act to inhibit the orienting reflex.

Repression impairs the process of perceptual scanning and, in so doing, curtails the total amount of relevant information available to the individual as a basis for effective behavior. A way of seeing is also a way of not seeing because when one focuses on object A, that involves a neglect of object B. As Dollard and Miller state, then, "Repression interferes with the neurotic's higher mental processes and prevents him from using these effectively in solving his emotional problems" (Dollard and Miller 1950).

3) They are precognitive.

In the case of subceptual repression, the cues are entirely autonomic (motor- emotional). In the case of perceptually-cued repression, autonomic responses are evoked by cognitive cues, but such cues are too distant from the actual repressed-content to be consciously related to it in any significant sense.

4) They are unmediated by the sort of symbolic processes involved in typical goal- seeking behavior and are therefore pre-volitional as well.

In other words, they are pre-cognitive in the usual sense of entailing a cognitive encounter which is subsequently suppressed or denied (as by Freud's contentious psychic "censor" in the unconscious mind).

5) They are cued by anticipatory-responses.

Behavioral responses closely associated with rewards and punishments are more highly reinforced than those more distant from rewards and punishments. They tend to become stronger than the more distant responses and to crowd these responses out by occurring earlier in the sequence. If, for example, an act has been experienced as extremely threatening, that behavior which has occurred in proximity to such an act becomes emotionally contaminated by association, and, other things being equal, contact with such behavior will prove sufficient to elicit precisely that sort of avoidance (flight) which was originally attached to the situation-proper. If such avoidance, based upon motor-emotional cues with respect to what might occur at a later phase in the sequence of behavior, is successful in eliminating subsequent punishment, it will be reinforced and will be even more likely to recur on subsequent occasions. The original response-sequence will, in effect, be short-circuited by repression.

6) Once established, repressions are strengthened and therefore sustained in two ways: (a) by the reinforcements associated with diminished anxiety (i.e., by the positive consequences accruing to the avoidance of anticipated punishments) and (b) by the positive consequences accruing to whatever substitutive course of action has been adopted in lieu of the original repressed tendencies.

In a sense, the difference between a **subceptual** response that elicits repression and **perceptual anticipations** that do likewise are essentially differences of degree rather than kind. They are both pre-cognitive and pre-volitional in nature. They are both cued by anticipatory responses that shape the normal orienting processes that occur in the subsequent perceptual processes. Perceptual anticipations that block perception on the basis of higher autonomic responses may be "perceived" as a vague intimation of potential threat that would be experienced if one were to pursue the course of action normally implied by the cue. They have an entirely different relevance, however, than they would have if they were allowed to progress through the entire sequence of perceptual cues, terminating in physical or psychological distress. For these reasons, I prefer to use the term **subception** to incorporate both types of non-volitional, cognitive orienting-responses despite the fact that they are significantly different **types** of subceptual responses, those emotionally cued by prior perceptions that block a particular process of consciousness and those that block attention away from incipient perceptions of content that promises to arouse "negative emotional vibrations."

What most psychological speculation (with the possible exception of William McDougall's writings on and around this topic in the 1920s) tends to miss is that both perceptual anticipations and subceptual responses have **positive** as well as **negative** cognitive effects. Perceptual anticipation operates via a goal radiant effect. The closer the individual comes to the consummation of a positive experience that is directed through the reduction of a series of intervening cognitive/affective steps--the closer he comes to the closure of a sequence of goal-directed behaviors--the more intense and focused his attention becomes and therefore the greater the affective-release (pleasure) that is experienced at the termination of the sequence of action. In a similar sense, since man is naturally active and tension-reducing (pleasure-seeking), the avoidance of experience/behavior on the basis of autonomic responses to pre-cognitive cues does not eventuate any lessening of perception but in a redirecting of the perceptual processes to cues that evoke positive autonomic responses on the basis of prior experience and that are therefore far more than likely to evoke the same or similar responses in the situation-at-hand.

Phrased somewhat differently, then, it is clear that "subception" is not merely the key to perception but the key to all of the cognitive processes and, indeed, to mature "consciousness" viewed in its totality. In a very general sense, just as behavior generates experience in the first instance, so, in a more limited and psychological sense, emotional responses evoke cognitive responses in the first instance.

2. Subception II

The theory of subception is reminiscent in many respects of the famous James- Lange theory of emotions that was formulated in the late nineteenth century by American philosopher-psychologist William James and Danish psychologist Carl Lange. The James-Lange theory stated, in essence, that we perceive a situation and then respond to it physically, with our emotional response being essentially a secondary response that is elicited by our primary behavioral response rather than by a "perception" that caused the physical response to occur in the first place.

The James-Lange theory is frequently represented as follows:

Perception--The boy encounters a bear while walking in the woods.

Behavioral response--The boy flees from the bear in an immediate motor-muscular response to the perception.

Emotional response--The boy construes his response and his behavioral reactions by investing them with cognitive meaning: "My God, that was a bear. I could have been killed!"

Subception posits very much the same model, but it qualifies the James-Lange approach in several respects.

First, the James-Lange theory fails to pay sufficient attention to the affective state of the organism when it first encounters the stimulus. The subceptual point of view, on the other hand, stresses that the person who acts is in no sense passive at the time of acting but is, instead, engaged in an ongoing series of cognitive and emotional interactions with his surroundings. In other words, it holds that emotionality is a constant which is redirected by behavior, but which does not elicit behavior de novo. The organism is in a constant state of "adjusting" that defies any sort of final "adjustment" altogether (short of death). In this sense, the organism is in some state of hedonic/emotional excitation even in dreamless sleep, and it is probably the nature and course of this excitation that provokes the still little understood interplay of memory and imagination that characterizes the covert behavior that occurs in our dreams.

Second, the James-Lange theory appears to accept the dominant nineteenth century view that perception is formatively cognitive in nature. It does not subscribe to anything approximating the hedonic scanning (i.e., sign-recognition as prior to symbol-recognition) process of subception to explain the transition from subliminal to liminal consciousness.

Third, in common with most nineteenth (and most twentieth) century psychology, the James-Lange theory does not provide a convincing definition of what constitutes an "emotion." If one subscribes to the "felt thought" orientations of Rugg and Polanyi, it seems overwhelmingly likely that an "emotion" is essentially a sequence of motor-muscular behaviors elicited by a state of hedonic excitation (whether pleasurable or displeasurable in nature) that generates a complex set of electro-chemical reactions within the organism. These physical reactions, in turn, elicit both cognitive and "emotional" responses within the organism as a whole.

In a basic sense, all subceptual responses are intuitive (in a behavioristic sense) because they are both pre-conscious, and conative (motor-emotional) rather than cognitive in nature. They essentially represent the initial relationship between the "subjectivity" of the individual and the "given" situation that he finds himself confronted with.

Subceptual Theory of Emotion

Conation--ongoing purposive behavior

(engenders an)

Encounter with a problematic situation caused by some blocking of such purposive behavior

(giving rise to)

Intuitive subception--sign-responses to the problematic situation at hand

(which is mentally processed as)

Perception/cognition of the subceived stimulus (for example, the object subsequently construed as a "bear") accompanied by vague intimation of subsequent feelings associated with the imminent emotional-response (of intense fear)

(which eventuates in an)

Emotional response (fear) invoked by the interplay of the nature and strength of the negative subception, the nature and strength of the subsequent perception, and the motor-muscular/electro-chemical feedback from behavioral responses which concurrently alter and frequently augment the initial perception of the stimulus. For example:

Activity--Hiking in the woods
Stimulus--Bear
Behavioral response--Flight
Emotional response--Fear
Cognitive response--"My God, that was a big bear. He could have killed me!"

Activity--Hiking in the woods
Stimulus situation--Bear in the woods
Subception
    Excitation
    Hedonic scan
    Hedonic focus (figure-ground relationship)
Behavioral response (autonomic reflex arc)--fright

Emotional response--motor-muscular behavior accompanied by electro-chemical emotionality
Cognitive response
Redirection of subsequent activity--Hiking in a direction away from the bear.

The nature and intensity of the "proto-emotions" of pleasure and pain determine what aspect of a given situation will constitute the stimulus within the overall situation that is being attended to. This stimulus, in turn, engenders the behavior response--which, in turn, elicits the cognitive/emotional reaction.

The nature of the pursuant emotion would appear to be contingent on nine things:

1) the nature (whether pleasure or pain), degree, and duration of the subceptual hedonic processes that elicited perception;

2) the nature, sequence and interplay of the pursuant motor-muscular and electro- chemical responses within the organism;

3) the interactions between component motor-muscular/electro-chemical reactions within an overall emotional response-set;

4) the interaction of a particular emotional response with the emotional response-set of the organism that prevailed at the time such a response was evoked;

5) the interaction of the particular emotional response with other emotional responses elicited by it and therefore experienced in conjunction with it;

6) the proportion of the response that is directly behavioral as opposed to that which is cognitive (and therefore only indirectly behavioral);

7) the extent to which an emotional response is compatible with concurrent or closely related emotional-responses (which might generate "interference states" such as those frequently described as "ambivalence" or "ambiguity";

8) the nature of the associated cognitive responses and the extent to which these responses generate either complementary or

competitive organic responses (which have their own peculiar resonances) within the overall "feelings" associated with the predominant response-pattern; and

9) whether and to what extent the entire interaction of organismic responses generates singular Gestalt qualities of experience (feelings) that function together to generate singular "emotional" responses which are experienced as substantially different than any of their component parts.

Even this is a partial list of the elements that might constitute a particular emotional-response. It does, however, serve to indicate the tremendous complexity of emotional responses. At basis, however, an "emotion" is always a unique pattern of hedonic responses channeled through a variety of different motor-muscular/electro-chemical behaviors that were initially elicited by a subceptual (hedonic) response to a precognitive sign that was scanned and invested with "relevance" by the character-structure of a particular subject (i.e., by the emotional/cognitive programming that constitutes the personal identity of the individual at hand). In the sense that all thought evolves into behavior of some sort, an emotion is a "feeling," but it is certainly not a "feeling" in any simple sense of the term.

How the subceptual hedonic-scan occurs on a preconscious level is a matter for conjecture at this point in time, because very little scientific inquiry has been directed at this matter. Assumedly, sensory input is processed in the pleasure-pain centers in the lower brain (presently viewed as centered in the hypothalamus) which gauges the nature and degree of stimuli that register above a certain threshold of intensity, with those below a certain threshold not being processed. Assumedly, stimuli eliciting mixed (pleasure and pain) potential are subjected to some sort of hedonic calculus (on a purely neurological level) to arrive at an "algebraic sum" experienced as basically either positive (pleasureful) or negative (painful) on the basis of their positive and negative valences. Possibly sequences of potential stimuli would be organized as potential subceptual "objects," providing that they possess sufficient hedonic impact to qualify as potential candidates for perception and providing that the conative process and the stimulus-situation remain sufficiently stable over a period of time to allow a sequence of subceptions/perceptions to occur.

Other things being equal, and assuming that some such process occurs, significant negative stimuli would probably take subceptual precedence over equally intense positive stimuli, because, in line with the psychobiological hierarchy of prepotency, incipient threats to survival and safety (which might be termed "paradoxical negatives," because they provide positive *knowledge* necessary to avoid negative *experience*) would take subceptual priority over equally intense stimuli which signify potential pleasures, and so on, in some sort of affective relationing-process. (In other words, assumedly, subception like perception, is organized around something approximating Maslow's hierarchy of prepotency. Other things being equal, those things necessary for safety and survival elicit more intense hedonic responses and command more attention, than those things that are merely desirable, and more intense desires associated with ego needs (usually pertaining to power and personal efficacy) ordinarily take priority over the less imperative values (from the point of view of the non-actualizing person) pertaining to the development of more complex and subtle types of cognitive and creative behavior.

Needless to say, all of this occurs with amazing rapidity, literally in a fraction of a second, with all significant stimuli organized pre-consciously in a response-hierarchy on the basis of their hedonic impact on the subjectivity of the actor.

In a very general sense, there would seem to be two basic types of subception operating simultaneously: what might be termed external subception, where the individual scans his outer environment of physical objects and events, and internal subception, where he scans his internal environment for images and ideas associated with the external stimuli at hand. In all probability, external and internal subceptions occur more or less simultaneously, and the subsequent perception is a product of the interplay between both processes as they interact with the directive process of intuitive conation.

Phrased somewhat differently, subception applies equally to objective and subjective stimuli. The personal past, like the present, is scanned subceptually on the basis of potential pleasure and pain. Memory is always a product of active reconstruction. Even fantasy is an imaginative reconstruction of experience on the basis of the remembered past. Most cognition is the interplay of memory, intentionality (based on memories of past gratifications) and present circumstances (guided by existing intentions that are themselves a product of past experience).

The relationship between subception and repression is interesting to consider. In the sense that all subception is a competition between sensed stimuli in which the most prepotently pleasurable stimulus (as either an end, means, or both) wins out, all subception could be viewed as a type of repression in a totally non-Freudian sense. On the other hand, viewed from a more traditionally Freudian sense of repression--that is, repression viewed as a volitional avoidance of psychological content that is incipiently threatening (painful) and therefore "censored" out of consciousness--subceptual theory differs in several important respects. Specifically, (1) it holds that avoidance is not "volitional" but rather caused by prevolitional sign-responses to precognized stimuli on the basis of purely hedonic reactions, and (2) it holds that such avoidance is caused fundamentally by means of selective subception based upon a sense of incipient threat evoked either directly (emotionally) or indirectly (as a type of knowledge) by the content at hand.

To make matters even more complicated, perception elicits, and is directed by, further subceptual processes in order to bring about the most meaningful cognitive focus. There are probably sequences of such subceptions which occur virtually instantaneously and which, like individual frames in a motion picture, are never experienced as events at all but merely as part of the overall perceptual/cognitive process. Thus, if I stand on a bill overlooking the ocean, I may *subceive* what I subsequently come to *perceive* as a house. I may subceive the house, in turn, *associationally* (horizontally) as similar to my memory of my grandmother's house in the country that I remember from childhood, *synthetically*, as a member of a class of houses--say Cape Cod style houses--or *analytically*, by zeroing in on one of the components of the house, say a window with light blue curtains. Any or all of these subceptions may occur, and any or all may elicit perceptions, which are then subceptually transformed into other perceptions, and so on. Since the internal environment of memory is selective on the basis of prior emotional reinforcements of experience, internal subception of images, ideas and such is necessarily very complicated. Not only are memories subceived but memories of imagined events (fantasies) are also subceived. Not only is conscious memory subceived, but preconscious memory (that which is remembered but temporarily unavailable for recall, like the maiden name of your grandmother or verb conjugations in French) are also potentially available for subception even when they are not available for conscious recognition. The unconscious--that which is actively kept out of conscious awareness--is actively suppressed by subceptual avoidance (based on "felt" motor-muscular intimations of threat) which denies it access to perceptual reality.

In subception, then, a preperceptual "emotional scan" determines whether and to what extent particular aspects of the physical and psychological content presented by a particular situation will be available to cognitive awareness. Subception is tacitly rational and therefore potentially intelligible, because it is controlled volitionally by the imperatives of intuitive behavior which was itself determined by the prior hedonic effects of previous behavior as this is, in turn, reflected in the character structure of the individual who is doing the responding. Phrased somewhat differently, intuitive behavior that is directed by subception does have a significant cognitive component, but this is latent. It is tacitly meaningful, but this meaning is largely after-the-fact, a corollary of ongoing behavior more than a determinant of it.

What an individual comes to believe on the basis of such intuitive behavior is therefore personally *meaningful* but it is not necessarily *true*. Whether the affective feedback from a person's behavior generates knowledge that is *objectively* true in the sense that it reflects the real nature and conditions of the world and not merely a warped and subjective response to it, depends on two basic conditions: (1) whether the individual perceives himself "situationally" as a part-function of a process of experience far broader than his narrowly conceived ego-needs (that is, whether he is growth-motivated); and (2) whether and to what extent he has been able to incorporate the need for objective understanding of self and world into his dominant value-orientation (as occurs in the case of autonomy).

From the empirical naturalist point of view, existentialism is both partly right and partly wrong. It is right in holding that man creates meaning in the world through his choices. It is wrong in failing to comprehend that these choices are largely the product of a self-system that is itself the product of pre-subjective, motor-emotional conditioning in response to a set of "given" conditions. In this respect, and as stated before, once personality has emerged, truth is subjective. But subjectivity is itself relative to conditions--the nature of man and the nature of the world--which are not "relative" in the final analysis at all but absolute and unchanging. Initially, the individual is an active entelechy, a blind and only tacitly intelligible conation. (Even Pavlov recognized that the dog could only be conditioned to respond on the basis of an "unconditioned stimulus" (hunger) which was not previously conditioned but rather innate.) As a child becomes more conscious of his surrounding world, he becomes volitional. As he becomes cognitive, his volition becomes the core of his emerging personality.

In this sense, a man becomes a separate self--and therefore self-determining ("free") before he becomes operationally rational. Indeed, he "chooses" long before he comprehends the *meaning* of his own choices. What he is not "free" to do (as yet) is to determine the volitional (subjective) bases for his own choices, to redefine his own character- structure volitionally. This is an option that only becomes possible in the case of autonomy.

Self-actualizing individuals are good subceivers because their subjectivity is characteristically transparent. Their self-systems tend to reflect learning which is based on the affective (pleasure-inducing) consequences of past behavior, so such learning has been verified pragmatically by its own affective consequences in the past.

Self-actualizers have realistic values that translate into realistic problems that are, in turn, relevant to the realistic (objective) situations that self-actualizing individuals tend to be attuned to. This gives rise to accurate subception, which generates accurate perception, and so on, in the usual cycle of positive synergism which has already been discussed.

For the self-actualizing individual in the highest (autonomous) mode of growth- motivation--the high-high orientation discussed earlier--the cognitive flow from conation to subception to perception to behavior and then back to conation again goes so continuously, so rapidly, and with so little interference that it assumes an almost aesthetic quality--a sense of being in fundamental harmony with the non-self (a sort of "lightness of being" to use Kundera's phrase). In some instances, this allows the self-actualizing person to function in a relatively straightforward, intuitive manner with very little recourse to the full cycle of emotional and cognitive steps that ordinarily occur in the process of normal problem-solving behavior. In such cases, the individual tends to go from conation to subception to perception (which virtually always includes some perceivable emotional intimations of the feelings and thoughts that would be subsequently evoked by continuing behavior in the full-blown emotional/cognitive response-cycle) and then back to mainstream conation with little or no "cognition" occurring at all in the usual sense of the term.

Non-self-actualizing people, on the other hand, tend to have an exaggerated and distorted subjectivity that interferes with the hedonic identification of stimuli in encountered situations. This short circuits the accuracy of their subsequent perceptions as well as the effectiveness of their pursuant behavior in the overall response-cycle. When this occurs, it tends to be the product of one of three processes: (1) subceptual repression (the hedonic avoidance of selected stimuli that signal imminent displeasure); (2) subceptual projection, where the individual conatively construes stimuli in a manner conducive to his own prepotent subjective requirements; or (3) subceptual ambivalence, which is caused primarily by interference between competing response-tendencies (values) that elicit a significant degree of static (or hedonic ambiguity) in the subceptual process.

In a sense, we all live backwards, projecting values that are nothing less than generalized memories of past gratifications which we seek to re-experience in the future by reinvoking past goals and attempting to realize these by reinstating past patterns of behavior that have been successful in attaining such goals. If we become a self in large part by imitating others, we remain a self in large part by imitating ourselves (with circumstantial variations) ad infinitum. In this sense, the old adage that "character is fate" is quite true. The fact that we are not invariably successful in reliving the high points of our past lives does not destroy the project of self-recovery that we are all embarked upon, because we learn more effectively when our motivation is heightened by some degree of frustration. Occasional failures in our attempts to relive our lives merely make us more determined to do so. It makes the reinforcements that we receive through our ongoing behavior even more reinforcing when they do occur.

In this sense, a significant aspect of personality is the fact that it serves as a sort of life-script which determines both what we seek in the future and also what we remember about our own past, because both future and past exist only cognitively on the basis of selective intentionality in the present. In this respect, personality induces a sort of autohypnosis in which the personal mythology of self and world created by our past experience inevitably drives us to live in such a way as to fulfill our own personal requirements. We strive to become what we *must be* on the basis of what we *are* which is a product of what we *were*--which was, in turn, determined primarily by presubjective actions that we had no control over at all in the first instance.

There are only three ways to combat this self-induced trance:

1) We can attempt to avoid it altogether by providing the sort of self-actualizing conditions in infancy and childhood that allow the individual to relate to reality-as-it-is and therefore to introject an objective-subjectivity like that which occurs in the case of autonomy.

2) We can attempt to counterindoctrinate the individual by making his personality inoperative as an effective means of realizing positive emotional gratification and then subjecting him to motor-emotional reconditioning on a directly behavioral basis that will terminate in a radically different sort of self-system (the sort of thing that occurs in the sort of behavioral therapy which was central to the kind of "thought reform" programs that were particularly prominent in some parts of the Communist world about a generation ago).

3) We can attempt to encourage the individual to cognitively reconstruct his own basic beliefs and values on the basis of a worldview that is fundamentally compatible with reality-as-it-is (as occurs in certain types of cognitive therapy).

The average person is not only susceptible to hypnosis. He lives in a state of hypnotic trance. He has been internally programmed with a subjectivity that was determined by an extended state of suggestibility (active sentiency) in which his experience was dictated by his behavior, which was, in turn, determined by his circumstances.

True freedom occurs only when a person becomes capable of transcending the nonrational and, generally, irrational character-structure indoctrinated into him during the earliest years of life by "transvaluating" his most basic beliefs and values. Such a person can be characterized in five ways:

1) He has recognized and affirmed reality as-it-is, attaining a sort of "ontological lucidity" which is based upon an empirical naturalistic worldview.

2) He has achieved a fundamental sense of self-understanding--a sort of "psychological lucidity." He knows who he is and what he believes.

3) He has reconciled his personal beliefs with his concept of reality. He is comfortable with and adapted to the world as-it-is.

4) He has formulated a course of action consonant with both his personal beliefs and with the nature of the world in which he lives. This course of action provides him with the opportunity for the fullest expression of that sort of rational commitment that is designed to maximize personal happiness and, in so doing, help him fully realize his potentialities as a particular person over an optimum period of time.

5) He has, in all of these ways, become truly "free" in the sense of being fully "self-determining," because he realizes that the traditional ego-self is essentially an illusion, that true freedom lies in recognizing the necessary interdependence of all Being and working actively for the realization of the larger and all-encompassing Self in a process of positive synergy (in which objectivity promotes personal effectiveness, which generates pleasure, and thereby reinforces objectivity, and so on).

Subception/Freedom
Ongoing personal behavior
    (is directed by means of)
Intuitive conation
    (which is, in turn, directed by)
Subception--a hedonic sensory scan (a sort of preperceptual radar) that determines what stimuli shall be attended to at any particular moment
    (which precedes all)
Perception, or cognitive interpretation of sensory-input
    (which is continuously and progressively refined through the higher processes of)
Cognition
    (which terminates, in part, as an)

Overall system of belief

(which modifies the)

Entire process of subsequent ongoing behavior in a direction consonant with its own assumptions--and so on, in a circular and self-confirming cycle.

Subception and Free Choice

The nature of man and the nature of the world dictate that a person responds hedonically to the consequences of his own behavior, learning directly or indirectly, only on the basis of pleasurable consequences.

Since human nature is a constant, while individual situations differ radically, the earliest circumstances are basic in determining character-structure (personality). Other things being equal, however, once character has evolved and taken form, character predominates over circumstances in determining subsequent changes in the character- structure of the individual so the character-structure becomes increasingly the product of selective perception as time goes on.

This character-structure operates through subception on the basis of ongoing behavior generated by its own imperative needs. It makes perceptions/cognitions available only on an after-the-fact basis as determined by preperceptual hedonic scanning that is guided by an individual's overall intentional (conative/normative) orientation which, as a product of prior hedonic reinforcement, shapes memory (and therefore intentionality itself, which is ultimately rooted in memory) to conform to existing character-structure.

The Emergence of Autonomy

Pure conation--the organism as active structure-function before postnatal learning has occurred

is usually experienced as

Preperceptual unity--a continuation of the prenatal cycle of deprivation-eliciting- gratification in which there is more or less continuous parental intervention to support need-gratification during infancy.

This evolves into

active sentiency--the infant's innate need for active behavior gives rise to sensory excitation caused by responses to external stimuli as well as by interruptions and delays in the deprivation-gratification cycles.

This eventuates in the

earliest motor-emotional learning which is based on the direct hedonic consequences of ongoing behavior, constituting a sort of approach-avoidance learning with little or no intervening subjectivity.

This develops into

cognitive associational learning based on (1) the identification of stimuli with pleasure or pain; (2) the internalization of images/signals/symbols elicited by such stimuli; (3) the identification of the same and similar reinforced stimuli with each other--matching of patternalities within stimuli--and the internalization of such identifications as the first metaphorical concepts (for example, "all furry objects are cats"); (4) the identification of the same and similar patterns of behavior (processes) as the first analogical concepts (for example, grasping behaviors generalized as "grasping," an instrumental tool-concept; or the internalization of "cause-and-effect" as a general explanatory principle; and (5) proto-volition--pre-symbolic, non-cognitive sign-learning, guided by remembered images of previous hedonic encounters with the same and similar objects and events--the beginning of subception.

This evolves into

holistic associational learning--the association of object-concepts (metaphors) and process-concepts (analogies), evolving into still larger concepts and meta-concepts in which perceived constancies and continuities between concepts are grouped into larger and more abstract concepts.

This ultimately leads to

self-consciousness--a subjective sense of self as a separate entity in relationship to others and in relationship to the environment in general--including a recognition of others as metaphorical selves that are essentially similar to one's own self.

This leads to the

metaphorical identification of self with significant others and the imitation of others as a guide to personal behavior.

This generates a
redefinition of self on the basis of the identification with and imitation of significant others.

This contributes toward the
growth and development of perception, cognition and volition on the basis of the emerging symbolic (abstract) awareness of self, others, and the surrounding world.

This generates a
symbolic separation of "isness" and "oughtness"--including a clearer distinction between self-concept as a descriptive entity and self-ideal as a prescriptive entity.

This leads toward an increasingly complex symbolism at abstract levels resulting in a general concept of reality as well as a general concept of self on both the cognitive and normative levels of operation, as well as an increasingly satisfactory synthesis of both of these, terminating in a fully-functioning and directive personality-system that serves as the cognitive "program" for subsequent behavior.

All of this may eventuate in a sort of meta-cognition--the systematic analysis and reevaluation of existing beliefs about self and world on the basis of objective intellectual criteria that go beyond the particular content of the existing personality and that therefore provide the basis for reformulating the previously dominant worldview and replacing it with one that is essentially compatible with reality-as-it-is--which is essentially what autonomy based upon self-actualizing growth-motivation is all about.

3. Pleasure and Happiness

The highest psychological good is pleasure. Pleasure is an electro-chemical response within the central nervous system that is elicited naturally through the equalizing of physical (motor-muscular) tensions within the organism.

Both pleasure and pain centers have been discovered in the limbic system of the hypothalamus in the lower brain. Research in the electrical stimulation of the brain indicates that it is possible to invoke both pleasure and pain responses directly by transmitting electrical stimulation to these centers by placing electrodes into the appropriate areas of the brain. The nature of the electro-chemical responses that are evoked are not well understood at this time, and the whole topic of electro-chemical stimulation of the pleasure and pain centers is an exceedingly complicated one that goes significantly beyond the scope of this book.

There are physical pain responses--such as those that are evoked by placing one's hand in a flame--that are essentially reflexive in the sense of being direct, intense and initiated basically by means of preconscious stimulus-response arcs <u>within the spinal</u> cord or in the lower brain centers. These occur without any sort of cognitive mediation. There are probably somewhat analogous reflexive or semi-reflexive pleasurable responses such as those invoked by sucking in the newborn that may be similar to the reflexive pain responses in the sense that they are essentially non-cognitive stimulus-response connections that are "wired into" the central nervous system at birth. These too are not well understood to date.

For present purposes, the term "pleasure" is used with reference to cognitively processed experience that indirectly yields a "positive" sense of tension-reduction (or, in some cases, tension-*production*, where the basic problem relates to an insufficient degree of tension to generate "pleasurable" tension-reduction). In all events, the biodynamics of pleasure and pain, while fascinating, go well beyond the confines of the present discussion except in the very broadest sense.

The logical *contrary* of pleasure is *pain*. The logical *opposite* of pleasure is *nonpleasure*. Since all human experience is hedonically charged with some degree of pleasure or pain (or some combination of the two), there is no such thing as a literal state of "non-affect" in a conscious organism. What is referred to as a "non-affective" state is actually one in which the degree of hedonic involvement is very slight, shifting imperceptibly around an emotional baseline that vacillates only in the most marginal sense from positive (pleasurable) to negative (displeasurable) responses.

The question of what constitutes the affective baseline--the state of emotional equilibrium between pleasure and pain--is necessarily vague and must therefore be approached with caution. It differs according to the emotional slate of the individual who is undergoing emotional excitation as well as to the surrounding field of stimuli that the individual is responding to. Assumedly, however, any person at any particular time has a dominating sense of affective involvement with the surrounding world that largely determines whether and to what extent he will be stimulated in a positive or negative manner by any new experience. If these dominating senses of affective involvement were to be mathematically averaged in some way over a significant period of time, we would have something approximating a mean state of affective excitation that would constitute a rough state of affective equilibrium for the individual in question.

Pleasure is not a state but a process. "Psychological pleasure," since we are primarily concerned with conscious or "perceived" experience and not with simple emotional reflexes, is the response elicited by cognitive (psychological) processes that generate more basic biological responses of a positively hedonic sort in the lower centers of the brain.

The human being has a predefined physical structure that is proactive. It seeks from the very beginning of life to function in such a way as to realize its possibilities for action in order to resolve the tensions implicit within this physical structure as it relates to the equally predetermined structure of the physical world. The world which surrounds the human being is also teleologically evolving according to the stresses implicit within the continuously interactive subcomponents that make up its own broader and more encompassing nature.

Ontologically, the world is constantly changing in response to its own internal requirements. These requirements emerge out of its own determinative structure-function (which includes man and human culture as two significant aspects) that is inextricably bound up in the total process of emergent evolution in which what *was* inexorably interacts to create what *is*, which unavoidably generates what *will be* through the process of infinitely complex (and, therefore, intellectually indeterminable) cause-and-effect relationships.

In the course of personal development, implicit human needs are cognitively associated with certain objects and events in the surrounding world. These associations, once psychologically assimilated, are ultimately translated through more advanced cognitive processes into goals (which are, in turn, often generalized into abstract values--which are essentially classifications of goals). Human beings experience pleasure as the active resolution of perceived tensions that are generated by the resolution of problems, which are, in turn, generated by difficulties (conflicts) engendered by the pursuit of goals.

Since a *goal* is, by definition, that which a person does not possess arid seeks to acquire, the attempt to gratify a need by attaining a goal generates conflict relating to the conditions that must be addressed in the attempt to attain the goal and to subsequently resolve the state of need which elicited activity in the first place. The perception of the condition that blocks the goal-seeking process constitutes the perception of the *problem*.

When the problem is effectively resolved and the goal is attained, the resolution of tensions is experienced subjectively (through electro-chemical responses within the central nervous system) as *pleasure*. Conversely, the failure to resolve the problem--whether through lack of action or through ineffective action--generates a sort of "psychological pain" (the negative, displeasurable hedonic state frequently referred to in psychological literature as "frustration").

If pleasure is an epiphenomenon of tension-reduction, *tension* as such is not necessarily a negative phenomenon. On the contrary, there are essentially two types of tension: *productive tension and counterproductive tension.*

Productive tension energizes the organism and propels it into action. In the normal need-gratification sequence that occurs in the course of personal development, the more compelling needs generate productive tensions toward types of behavior that elicit problems. These problems, if effectively resolved, lead to higher and more heuristic needs, each generating pleasure and providing the basis for future pleasurable acts directed toward subsequent need-gratifications at increasingly more complex levels of personal behavior.

Counterproductive tensions, on the other hand, emerge largely from unfulfilled or distorted deficiency needs that frequently lead to warped perception and behavioral rigidity. The deficiency-motivated person, for example, suffers from counterproductive tensions that force him to attend to compelling subjective requirements that are not generally relevant to the situation at hand--that are not "realistic" in the context of the circumstances that prevail--and that generate a sell-perpetuating process of increasingly progressive pain and distress on a psychic level.

Someone once said that *neurotic anxiety* sterns from having significant psychological problems that one cannot solve, while *existential anxiety* sterns primarily from "meaninglessness," the lack of significant problems to solve. The distinction is a vast oversimplification, but it is partly on target. Existential anxiety is largely a problem associated with the individual's psychological engagement in the world, a problem of inadequate personal commitment to some personally significant course of action which can serve as a mode of overall response. In this sense, existential anxiety is largely a sin of *omission* rather than one of *commission*. It grows out of the individual's inability or unwillingness to commit himself to some course of action that provides a basis for the sort of productive tension that makes potentially pleasurable experience possible. It is largely a problem of problem-perception rather than of problem-solving.

The neurotic's problem, on the other hand, grows out of the type and degree of psychological tension (often associated with guilt or with deep-seated fears) that interferes with effective cognition (problem-solving) and that therefore tends to block any satisfactory, ongoing process of emotional adaptation by giving rise to the sort of counterproductive tensions that short circuit the sort of truly adaptive behavior which facilitates future adaptive behavior.

In order to experience pleasure, five basic conditions must occur:

1) The individual must seek to realize some perceived goal.

2) Attaining this goal must entail some sort of volitional (intended) action.

3) The perception of the goal, in conjunction with the perception of the sort of action that is required to attain it, must be blocked by some impediment that is perceived to exist within the encountered situation.

4) The problem as perceived must generate some idea about the kind of action necessary for its resolution.

5) The idea must be acted upon, generating hedonic consequences. If the idea works, the problem is resolved, the goal is attained, and some degree of pleasure (tension-reduction) is experienced. If not, the anticipated pleasure is not experienced, and counterproductive tension is exacerbated.

Phrased somewhat differently, then, at a purely psychological level, maximum pleasure requires six things:

1) a large quantity of

2) high quality (that is, difficult but not insurmountable) problems that

3) elicit a significant degree of tension that

4) can be effectively resolved on the basis of available behaviors, and that

5) go on to provide the basis for a subsequent redefinition of needs as well as related problems that are capable of generating still higher and more significant problems that

6) can become the source of still more pleasurable experience in the future and provide the emotional and cognitive basis for the sort of self-validating and self-confirming positive behavior that is the hallmark of growth-motivated behavior.

While the psychological requirements for any sort of pleasure to occur are in no sense suspended at this level of operation, they are supplemented by additional conditions that allow them to be incorporated into a total way of life that provides the sort of overriding behavioral context for optimizing pleasurable experience over the optimum period of time. In other words, before there can be any experience of pleasure the individual must be motivated to pursue some course of action. This action must create conflict with circumstances that block the immediate realization of that which is sought. This conflict must be resolved through some sort of effective behavior.

The more intensely concerned a person is with pursuing a particular course of action, the more intensely he experiences the pleasure elicited by resolving the problems entailed by whatever this course of action may be. Other things being equal, the more intensely committed a person is to following through on a particular course of action the more active he becomes and the more problematic the world is experienced to be. Motivation energizes the organism. The more motivated a person is the more he comes into conflict with his surroundings, and the more this conflict eventuates in consciousness, which is always ultimately a byproduct of conflict.

Other things being equal, the more intelligent a person is (in the sense that he has a heightened cognitive capacity to perceive the world symbolically and to manipulate such a symbolic world effectively through reason) the more rapidly he will be able to process information in the problem-perceiving and problem-solving processes that are the ultimate conditions for any significant degree of personal consciousness to occur. Such a person will perceive *more* problems than most others. He will also be able to solve such problems more quickly and effectively than others normally do.

Phrased somewhat differently, the more a person comprehends both *quantitatively* and *qualitatively*--that is, the more extensive his understanding of the world is and the more intensive (profound) this understanding is--the richer and more complex his interior (subjective) world of understandings and information will be. Accordingly, the greater his potential will be for relating to the external world through the instrumentality of his own directive psychological processes.

The more meaning a person comprehends, the more potentially meaningful (relevant) the world around him becomes. Such a person sees more meaning (relevance) in situations. He also sees more complex layers of meaning in situations. Unlike the average person, he is more likely to find problem-perception itself to be less "common sense" and more problematic, frequently discovering intellectual provocation in even the most ostensibly prosaic circumstances.

Since such a person has a fuller and more complex internal world, he is more capable not only of heightened consciousness but also of heightened *self*-consciousness. He is capable of perceiving his own values and beliefs, as well as reflecting on his own well-stocked memory banks, relating the external world of objects and events to his internal world of symbols and images, generating creative perceptions that go far beyond the possibilities that might ordinarily appear to be contained within the situation at hand.

Viewed *philosophically* (ontologically) rather than *psychologically*, the highest good is not *pleasure* per se but *happiness*. A "happy life" is, in essence, the sort of life in which the individual's behavior serves to initiate, sustain, and augment the optimum quantity and quality (intensity) of pleasurable-instances over the optimum period of time.

The term *optimum* is used in preference to *maximum* because, in many instances, present pleasure must be delayed or moderated in the cause of quantitatively or qualitatively greater pleasures in the future. In this sense, *happiness* is the cognitive organization of ongoing experience that seeks to optimize pleasure in the long run or on balance, and not merely to maximize it continuously without regard to the future. If maximum pleasure in the present were the summum bonum, drug addiction would be fully defensible as a moral choice. Since self-actualization operates both hedonically and cognitively to promote this goal, self-actualization enhances personal happiness and, in so doing, optimizes pleasurable experiences on a psychological level as well.

Actually, the *optimization*, of pleasure is the same as the *maximization* of pleasure for all practical purposes, because both nonpleasure and displeasure are necessary components of the pleasure-seeking process fully conceived. Certain types of displeasure (distress, frustration, and such) are psychological preconditions for the sort of tension- reduction which makes pleasure possible to begin with. In this sense, it is rather pointless to be particularly punctilious about making the distinction between *optimum* pleasure and *maximum* pleasure, because optimum pleasure would necessarily also lead to maximum pleasure under realistic conditions that imply a sufficient number and degree of nonpleasurable and unpleasurable experiences as the unavoidable psychological basis for the sort of affective contrast between nonpleasurable/displeasurable responses, on the one hand, and the kind of reactions to these that give rise to "pleasurable" experiences in the first place.

The same qualification can be applied to the use of the terms *optimum* and *maximum* when applied to the relationship between the pursuit of pleasure and the duration of life. If pleasure requires an active perceptual-symbolic relationing of experience that is processed electro-chemically within the central nervous system, the maximum duration of the pursuit of pleasure via happiness is necessarily based on two conditions: (1) whether and to what extent a person is capable of processing experience cognitively in order to experience a positive ratio of pleasure to pain in the long run or on balance, and (2) whether and to what extent the individual's central nervous system is capable of functioning in such a way as to electro-chemically process such a positive ratio of pleasure to pain.

What constitutes these conditions is necessarily difficult to pin down, but, in general, there would seem to be at least two situations in which personal happiness would be more or less precluded:

1) instances where the individual is psychologically disturbed to the extent that he is chronically unhappy in an extreme sense in which there appears to be very little likelihood of positive change (as appears to occur in certain aggravated sorts of negative behavioral synergy or in some instances of severe mental illness, whether organic or functional in nature), and

2) where the individual is afflicted with chronic physical pain that is prepotent over normal psychological processes (which are

themselves also ultimately *physical* processes) and blocks access to emotional gratifications of a normal sort.

If pleasure is contingent upon intellectual variables as well as on the ability and inclination to be vitally involved in significant projects of social change, it may be that senility itself would, under certain circumstances, create a sufficient degree of physical and intellectual disability to preclude "happiness" as a viable objective more or less altogether. Such a situation would effectively shift the hedonic balance in a predominantly negative direction. Life would become a process of chronic and essentially irreversible distress. If and when such a condition occurs, there would clearly be a potential argument for terminating a life which is no longer up to the task of optimizing pleasure and which, indeed, generates the type of pain or chronic psychological distress which would effectively block any satisfactory pursuit of happiness altogether. It can be argued that such a course of action--suicide, or whatever--becomes the only moral course of action that is defensible on empirical-behavioral grounds.

In contrast to being opposed to pleasure in the short term--and all pleasure is "short term" of necessity--the point of happiness, viewed as a way of life and not merely as a description of an electro-chemical event, is that happiness is a cognitive phenomenon and not merely a state of affect. Fully understood, happiness dictates that what is desirable in the long run is not pleasure as such but rather the sort of pleasure that guarantees the optimum quantity and quality of pleasure over the optimum period of time commensurate with any general pursuit of happiness as such.

The term *optimum* is used in place of the term *maximum* advisedly, because happiness qualifies the pursuit of pleasure in four fundamental ways:

1) It holds that the pleasurable experiences envisioned should not be self- terminating (like overdosing on lethal drugs or having a flagrant affair with the wife of the heavyweight champion).

2) It holds that pleasure should not be so potentially hazardous that it risks life and limb (and therefore seems likely to terminate or radically curtail the sort of conditions necessary to promote the *continued* pursuit of pleasure).

3) It holds that the sort of pleasure sought should not be likely to generate the sort of biological or psychological consequences that would markedly reduce the possibility of realizing effective pleasurable experiences in the future.

4) Finally, it maintains that the sort of pleasures sought should generally provide the basis for a positive synergism cycle in the course of subsequent behavior that will enhance the future pursuit of pleasurable experiences by reinforcing all of the personal characteristics--both intellectual and emotional--that provide the psychological foundations for the maximum realization of pleasure in the first place.

One of the paradoxes of pleasure is that the quantity and quality of pleasurable experiences alters the affective base and therefore effectively raises the ante on the nature of subsequent pleasurable responses that are required to invoke the same or similar sorts of pleasurable responses on subsequent occasions. An experience that is exciting and highly pleasurable the first time around is less likely to be so on repetition. As the old saying goes, "Nothing fails like success."

In other words, a surfeit of pleasure in one realm of experience means that even more intense pleasures will be required to stimulate an equivalent state of pleasurable affect in that same realm of experience on subsequent occasions (particularly if they occur in rapid succession) or that significantly different sorts of pleasure will be needed to establish some sort of "affective contrast" with those previously undergone. In short, pleasure exists on a gradient. Other things being equal, the greater the experienced tension or deprivation, the greater will be the pleasure generated by the sense of tension-reduction. In this sense, then, and as already remarked, problems (conflicts) may block pleasure in an immediate sense, but they are a necessary precondition for any sort of pleasurable experience to occur at all, when viewed in total context.

From the broader philosophical point of view, then, the psychological "pleasure principle" must be qualified in two fundamental ways. First, it must be adapted to the fact that certain pleasures are extremely gratifying precisely because of the gradient of tension to tension-reduction (the severity of the contrast) that is generated in the course of behavior. Nietzsche talked quite cogently about the imperative of "living dangerously." Doing something risky, from playing Russian roulette to risking a fortune at cards, can provide an almost unparalleled sense of excitement that can eventuate in consuming sorts of pleasure. But they may also backfire. One may be killed, bankrupted or otherwise devastated by the consequences of extreme risks that fail.

In a similar sense, cocaine or heroin may provide sources of exhilarating pleasure in an immediate sense, but, utilized frequently or over extended periods of time, they are quite likely to destroy the physical and psychological conditions required for effective behavior in the long run and therefore for the realization of optimum pleasurable experience in the long run as well.

"Happiness," then, is a *philosophical* concept and not merely the label attached to a subjective feeling like pleasure or pain. As such, happiness is a broader and more encompassing value than *pleasure*, because it provides a theoretical plan of action at the very highest level of abstraction for initiating, sustaining and promoting pleasure to the fullest extent possible. *Self-actualization* is, in a similar sense, a more encompassing value than happiness, because it goes even further beyond the purely psychological, addressing itself to the relationship that necessarily holds true between the psychological and the philosophical. What makes Maslow's concept of self-actualization so important is that it is a *psychological* theory that implicitly encompasses a *philosophical* point of view.

Happiness, as viewed here, sees pleasure as the only intrinsic value on a personal level. But a person can be happy--Hitler and Stalin may be possible examples--and still not be self-actualizing What the philosophy of self-actualization states is, in effect, that the ultimate psychological unit is not the organism but society and--be society as such--the total unity of encompassing Being. This Being-Gestalt is also teleologically unfolding in a continuous dialectic of implicit meaning.

In this sense, perhaps the most radical notion contained within self-actualization philosophy is the notion that not all meaning is "personal," that there is such a thing as "objective meaning" that transcends individual thought-processes altogether. In essence, the argument that the self-actualization philosophy advances in favor of such "objective knowledge" might be summarized as follows.

The world, like man, is naturally and continuously active. It is implicitly conative, because its activities are directed by the inherent structure of its component parts as well as by the unavoidable and equally structured cause-and-effect interactions that are continuously occurring between these different components as they try to effect a consummation of the total structure-function process (which is implicit within other structure-function processes and which engender new, ongoing and interaffecting types of structure-function) in the process of emergent evolution.

There is, in this sense, an ongoing (if intellectually indeterminate) teleological dimension to reality. It is intelligible to man to the extent that human intelligence is capable of assimilating the patternality inherent within the organized processes of nature. Nature, like man, seeks the equilibration of forces within the overriding processes of continuous change.

Man, as a unique energy-system contained within this all-encompassing energy-system, acts as a sort of cosmic cerebral cortex. He has the singular capacity to comprehend significant elements within the nature and direction of natural forces as well as both some of the principles that govern their interaction as well as their relationship to the whole.

Man also has the potential capacity to act upon these forces anthropocentrically (which is the social analogue of personal subjectivity), to seek to comprehend the world objectively (through growth-motivation and its highest expression of autonomy), and, in so doing, to discover whether and to what extent his own interests as one element within nature are compatible with the implicit nature and direction of the more encompassing forces that comprise the natural world as a whole.

It may be that, acting in complicity with nature in general, and looking upon it as the ultimate extension of personal selfhood (as occurs in self-actualization) is a more enlightened and effective course of action in the long run than attempting the far more formidable task of attempting to reconstruct nature to satisfy purely human needs.

Man's nature is, in one sense, to be unnatural, self-conscious. But, in self-actualization self-consciousness expresses itself as an awareness of absolute Being (objective reality), so the characteristic motive of the self-actualizing person is to become socially self-actualizing and, ultimately, cosmically self-actualizing. In this sense, self-actualization encourages cooperation rather than competition with nature.

As self-actualization philosophy sees it, the highest function of man lies in the realization of the individual's singular capacity for grasping the ultimate meaning of reality and for using this meaning to perfect himself, others, and the world in general. For the self-actualizing person, it is necessary to be happy, but it is not sufficient. "Personal happiness" is based on a cognitive short-sightedness that sees man as alienated from others and from reality in general. Man's highest happiness is to fulfill his most elevated potentialities, which are cognitive and which inexorably lead to a far broader concept of self--what might be viewed as the *objective* self--to a fusion of self and non-self (which is one aspect of autonomy), and, finally, to a creative expansion of consciousness itself directed toward transforming and realizing what Tillich has called "the ground of Being"--which is ultimately the highest consciousness of all, because it encompasses all of the conditions required for consciousness itself to occur.

Self-actualization occurs on two different levels. During infancy and childhood, fully functioning self-actualization is only potential. All "actualization" of the self at this time necessarily occurs at a deficiency-motivated level in response to lower-level biological and psychological needs. On the other hand, the developmental years are central to subsequent self-actualization. It is the deprivation and frustration of the deficiency-needs during the earliest years that creates the psychological disturbances (fixation, repression, regression, and such) that ultimately serve to block any significant degree of fulfillment in later years. In a sense, then, it is important to realize that successful deficiency-motivated behavior in the developmental years (and particularly during infancy and early childhood) provides the critical physical and psychological basis for later growth-motivation.

In general, only children whose deficiency needs have been effectively gratified at the proper time, and in the appropriate sequence and to a sufficient degree are destined to become viable candidates for self-actualization during their adult years. Only those children whose underlying sense of chronic need-gratification has become engrained as a more or less constant (and therefore "motivationally irrelevant") aspect of their reality orientation are likely to develop into growth-motivated, self-actualizing individuals in later life.

Once a person has successfully moved beyond deficiency motivated behavior and has become habituated to success in the course of his everyday experience, his prepotent deficiency needs continue but they become "psychologically invisible" as subjective determinants of behavior. Such a person develops a new type of motivation in which his central need is no longer the need to satisfy deficiencies but, rather, the need to structure his behavior and his experience in such a way as to generate the conditions-

-the sort of goals, problems, and ways of dealing effectively with these- -that will allow him to experience the same sort of pleasures that were previously elicited by deficiency-motivation but that are now experienced on a *post*-deficiency level in a totally different way. The individual's new and now dominant need becomes the need to project and pursue the kind of personal meaning within the world that will allow him to create the kind of psychological tensions that are necessary to sustain and advance the kind of tension-reductions (pleasures) which are preconditions for a fully realized process of positive and self-confirming synergistic behavior to unfold.

Put in somewhat different terms, such a person no longer "needs" anything in particular, but he does have a pervasive and continuing need for the sort of life-style that can serve as the basis for productive new needs that are a generic requirement for the subsequent need satisfactions that are capable of generating pleasurable experience in a post-deficiency world. From the point of view of the ordinary deficiency-motivated person--who comprises the vast bulk of any population--such needs may appear to be gratuitous because they are not required to address the lower and more basic imperatives of physical and psychological survival. In a sense, the self-actualizing person has shifted gears. He has moved out of the lower gears of deficiency-motivation and into a sort of psychological overdrive. He is now "cruising" in a slate of "meta-motivation" (which Maslow terms "growth motivation") where his over-riding commitment is precisely directed toward defining and pursuing an overriding commitment which is adapted to the needs of his highest nature. This highest need is, in this sense, to formulate some meaning in life, and then to pursue this meaning in such a manner that will allow him to re-experience the same sort of emotional gratification on a cognitive level that he previously experienced on a far less predictable basis when confronting the more primitive problems relating to physical and psychological survival in a less comprehensible world that was overwhelmingly characterized by danger and threat.

Since, he has already passed through the "identity-crisis" aspects of his life, during the love and ego-need levels of deficiency motivation, this

42

project does not ordinarily entail a radical redefinition of the self. The self-system--personal identity--already exists and functions to direct behavior, in the case of self-actualization, what changes radically is how this self-system *functions*.

If, for example, I am a boy who has been born into a family where my father and his father before him were both physicians, it is highly likely that I will, at least initially, tend to identify with them and also seek to become a physician. This will largely determine what I will study at school and will probably have a strong effect on structuring my interests. On the other hand the *program* of behavior that I embark on--its content--is less important than the *process* that it entails. I have made--albeit tacitly and not with a full awareness of that it implies--a commitment to a certain course of action in the world. I now have to do certain things in order to attain certain goals, in order to realize more fundamental ends.

By pursuing this course of action, I propel myself into creative conflict with my surroundings. The conflict implied by my commitments generates problems. These problems, in turn, dictate actions. The consequences of these actions generate emotional (and at a more molecular level, hedonic) responses. I am, in this sense, as fully alive as I was when I first encountered the world--but in a significantly different way.

Since I am now essentially growth-motivated, I am perceptually accurate. Since I am perceptually accurate, I am behaviorally effective. Since I am effective, my needs are characteristically gratified, and I experience the world as pleasurable. These effects are cumulative. Once I am self-actualizing, I see the world as-it-is, as a natural realm of being rooted in personal experience rather than as a configuration of metaphysical absolutes that inevitably determine who I am and what I should do.

My behavioral effectiveness is also symbolically transformed (and internalized) into a set of effective principles that govern my thinking (logic) as well as into the way in which I inquire into the world (which increasingly embraces scientific enquiry as well as other modified forms of experimental enquiry that lend themselves more readily to the more amorphous questions and the "sloppy data" that do not lend themselves to strict scientific verification procedures). Initially, however, in the earliest phases of self-actualization I don't *know* that I *know* these things. They can be inferred by others on the basis of my behavior, perhaps, but, for me, they remain vague and merely incipient understandings that exist largely on an intuitive basis rather than in the form of explicit, "theoretical" beliefs.

In other words, just as my reason evolved out of my growing awareness of constancies and continuities within my tacitly "reasonable" (but not actively "reasoned") behavior, which was established during the earliest months and years of life, my characteristic "objectivity" evolves out of the internalization of understandings that have been distilled out of my responses to a real world that I am capable of relating to with a bare minimum of subjective distortion but that I do not, as yet, fully comprehend on any explicit basis.

As I become more intellectual--more effectively cognitive both in how I think and in what I come to know--my understanding of my own identity also undergoes a radical change. I grasp the fact that, since I am a human being and since human beings are inherently rational, social, and (by logical implication) moral as well, I am also therefore properly concerned with the well-being of others and not merely with my own self- interests. As my understanding of this patternality broadens and deepens, I come to realize that I am not only a part-function of mankind but that mankind is, in turn, merely a part-function of a still larger pattern of Being which encompasses the entire natural world as an interrelated whole.

My concept of self becomes basically an extended concept, in which I view my *self* as merely one aspect of a far larger *self/non-self* totality that is also continuously active and, at the same time, evolving toward the actualization of its own purposes (purposes that are implicit within its own controlling dynamics). My sense of alienation from others as well as from the surrounding world begins to be replaced with a sense of fusion--with a sense of being part of that encompassing oneness which Eastern philosophies have labeled with such terms as *satori* or *Samadhi*. My sense of seeing the world as-it-is gradually merges into a subjective sense of being-in-the-world and being-through-the-world.

As I grow older and my self-actualizing behavior matures, the affective feedback from my own behavioral effectiveness reinforces my self-actualizing life-style. The cognitive feedback from my objective cognition broadens and deepens my understanding of reality-in-general. The world becomes increasingly more "intelligible" as I become increasingly more "intelligent." Gradually I attain a level of cognitive effectiveness that makes cognition itself pleasurable and therefore a value to be sought. In time this evolves into the passionate intellectual curiosity of "autonomy" in which the attempt to comprehend reality in general (including the "self" as one aspect of that reality) becomes the local value-orientation that pervades my entire life. To the extent that this occurs, the traditional distinction between *truth* and *value* begins to dissolve, because the attempt to comprehend *truth* has become the central and controlling *value* in my life. The passion to *be* has begun to function through an encompassing passion to *know*. When this occurs, the traditional and erroneous dichotomy between truth and value--G.E. Moore's well-known "naturalistic fallacy"--has been eliminated because the pursuit of objective truth--the understanding of reality as-it-is--has become the overriding value within my life.

Effective cognition leads inexorably to more and more profound cognitions which serve as the basis for more exacting problems that are capable of generating still higher levels of tension-reducing pleasure. In a strange variation of Lawrence Peter's well-known "Peter principle," which holds that everyone in an organization strives to rise until he reaches his level of incompetence, the self-actualizing person continues to strive after goals, only to redefine these goals and seek still more challenging goals in the course of seeking to realize his own cognitive limits. What ordinarily saves such a person from reaching his "level of incompetence" is the fact that the positive synergism cycle created by the self-actualization process serves to make him increasingly more competent with time and, accordingly, to raise his level of competence to successively higher levels as he grows older.

The self-actualizing person is happy primarily because he is cognitively accurate and therefore effective. Once he has attained emotional gratification on one level of activity, he redefines his goals in more cognitively exacting directions in order to have the sort of problems that possess enough hedonic potential to guarantee tension-reduction at increasingly higher levels than those to which he has become accustomed. In other words, once behavior has become psychologically identified with one type of behavior, this type of behavior tends to become progressively less satisfactory as a source of future pleasure because it is no longer *experienced* as a significant "need" and therefore ceases to serve as a satisfactory *motive* for action. in this sense, it is necessary for self-actualizers continuously to define new and exacting cognitive goals that entail new and more exacting problems if they are to re-experience even the same level of tension-reduction (pleasurable-experience) that was produced by previously successful (and previously pleasurable) sorts of behavior.

Fully functioning self-actualization inevitably leads to creativity. A self-actualizing person seeks to be fully alive as the sort of person that he is. In part, he achieves this by a type of objective knowing in which he sees reality for what it is. Because he seeks a certain *type of knowing* rather than a certain *set of answers*, he is capable of responding empathically to situations by sensing the implicit organization and direction of events-- their teleological meaning--more or less independent of his own "personal" intentions. This is not to say that he always and consciously seeks to advance "the natural flow of events," merely that he is capable of sensing it. Having grasped the situation-as-it-is, he is more effective in the situation whether he seeks to change it or to work in harmony with it.

Self-actualization is an operational definition of *happiness* which holds, in effect, that a person is happy when he has basically satisfied his biological needs as well as his "lower" psychological needs for security, love and recognition, and has progressed on to "higher" self-actualization needs that are fundamentally cognitive, esthetic, and creative in nature. The rationale for this is, in essence, that, until the lower biological and psychological needs have been basically gratified, physical and psychological tensions so significantly outweigh the gratifications to be obtained by whatever tension-reductions occur that the individual's behavior is disproportionately weighted in the direction of tension/pain/stress rather than in the direction of tension-reduction/pleasure.

Through a process of developmental need-gratification some individuals graduate to a significant degree of self-actualization. Once this occurs, the individual's needs are less "survival-oriented" (and therefore less contingent upon particular external circumstances) and are far more "self-determined."

In a general sense, a self-actualizing person has three overriding needs:

1) He needs to continue to respond to the world problematically--he needs to define goals that are capable of generating a satisfactory set of tension-producing and tension-reducing actions.
2) He needs to define goals that elicit the sort of problems that are capable of being solved (and therefore capable of evoking pleasure and not merely of augmenting tensions with little hope of resolution).
3) He needs to define goals/problems that are essentially heuristic in the sense that they generate the sort of experiences that lead to additional goals/problems on still higher levels of psychological functioning that, in turn, generate additional pleasures, and so on (in something approximating a positive synergism cycle within the course of ongoing behavior).

If these conditions are met, the individual is confronted with growth-motivated problems that can be solved and that, in being solved, generate subsequent growth motivated problems at still more challenging levels of behavior which can also be solved, and so on. The final consummation of this process is a state (or actually a sustained *process*) of self-actualization in which the individual exists almost exclusively at the level of growth-motivation, responding to significant cognitive problems that are effectively resolved in personal behavior and that provide the basis for the perception of still more significant cognitive problems in the future.

In a sense, then, operational happiness--defined as self-actualization--is founded upon certain conditions that extend beyond the fundamental gratification of deficiency needs. Since a human being is naturally active and motivated by the need for pleasure, which is a biological (hedonic) effect generated by tension-reduction in the course of ongoing behavior, the individual has an undeniable need to be involved in some sort of active doing.

Since all behavior beyond infancy and early childhood is motivated by need, in which projected goals are blocked by problems that require solutions in order for tensions to be resolved (and therefore for pleasure to occur), the individual *requires* problems in order to experience the pleasurable consequences of problem-solving. Ironic though it may be, human beings *need* problems in order to *solve* problems. Since man must behave in order to be alive and fully conscious, he requires a life that is actively and continuously problematic. And, equally significant, since all pleasure exists on a gradient, the greater the tension (the more significant the problem) the greater the pursuant tension-reduction (pleasure).

This leads to an interesting situation: Other things being equal, the *more* problems that a person has and the more *intense* these problems are experienced to be, the more incipiently pleasurable (and therefore "happy") such a person is likely to be. On the other hand, problems as such, while necessary, are not sufficient. The individual must be able to resolve these problems if he is to undergo the active process of *adjusting* (as opposed to the passive state of *adjustment*, which is a negative value) that is experienced as pleasure. In a sense, it is these conditions that provide the explanation for why *self-actualization* provides a particular definition of *happiness*.

Creativity as a co-factor of self-actualization is not creating something de novo, independent of determining circumstances. It is primarily a matter of perceiving different and otherwise unrelated aspects of reality in some new combination. The self-actualizing person is intrinsically creative for seven reasons:

1) He perceives reality as-it-is, perceives more of it, and perceives it in greater cognitive depth.

2) He is flexible; he is more interested in what things mean in wider contexts than he is in how they relate to his own narrowly defined needs.

3) He is playful--he enjoys looking at things differently because he has been conditioned by his own past experience to anticipate pleasure from new experience.

4) He is self-confident; he trusts his own judgment and therefore he has the courage to act in new and innovative ways.

5) He is psychologically available to new experience and actively seeks out such experience, because he has learned to anticipate success (and therefore pleasure) from new experience in the past.

6) He enjoys cognition and uses it as his primary mode of response in the world.

7) He is better equipped to see relationships, because he thinks effectively and has a large stock of internalized experiences that provide a firm basis for making new cognitive associations in the course of the creative process.

4. Intuition/Felt-Thought

Thought as Holistic

At basis, "every human act is felt as well as thought. It embraces both feeling and thinking. Every creative act is noetic and carries a 'sense of authority' " (Rugg 1963:44). In the words of Zen scholar Daisetz Suzuki: "Feeling is at the source of all human deeds, and not dialectical difficulties. Psychology comes first, then logic and analysis, and not vice versa" (Suzuki 1956:26).

In a sense, then, all thought is rooted in kinesthetic activity. In much the sense originally conceived by the ancient Greeks, there is a "common sense," a <u>consensus</u>, which consists of a body of preverbal (and preperceptual) experience dictated by common human responses to certain common human needs which are shared by everyone and which form the behavioral substratum for all higher cognition. It may indeed be, as McLuhan suggests, that "... <u>touch</u> is not just skin contact with <u>things</u>, but the very life of things in the <u>mind</u>" (McLuhan 108).

As Laurence Kubie points out in his book <u>Neurotic Distortion in the Creative Process</u>, the term <u>cognition</u> stems from the Latin verb <u>cogito</u> which has the etymological meaning "to shake together" while the term <u>intelligence</u> derives from the term <u>intelligo</u> meaning "to choose, or select,

50

from" (Rugg 1963:217-218). As Kubie indicates "...the 'cogito' component, i.e., the assembling of new combinations, is predominantly a <u>preconscious</u> process... whereas 'intelligo' is of necessity preponderantly <u>conscious</u> (although here too preconscious processes play an essential contributory and economizing role)" (Rugg 1963:218).

In a sense, the distinction is, as Kubie suggests, very similar to that ordinarily drawn between <u>intuition</u> and <u>analytic thought</u>. <u>Analytic thought</u> typically entails division and selection. <u>Intuition</u>, on the other hand, is characteristically a "shaking together," an identification with, and participation in, the total requirements of the overall situation. Such a view of intuition succeeds, in Polanyi's words, in "merging our awareness of a set of particulars into our focal awareness of their joint particulars" (Polanyi 1960:44).

"By intuition [states Rugg] is meant the kind of <u>intellectual</u> <u>sympathy</u> by which one places one's self within an object in order to coincide with what is unique in it and consequently inexpressible. Analysis, on the contrary, is the operation which reduces the object to elements already known, that is, to elements common both to it and other objects. To analyze, therefore express a thing as a function of something other than as a translation, a development into symbols, a representation taken from successive points of view from which we note as many resemblances as possible between the new objects which we are studying and others which we believe we know already. In its eternally unsatisfied desire to embrace the objects around which it is compelled to turn, analysis multiplies without end the number of its own points of view in order to complete its always incomplete representation, and ceaselessly vanes its symbols that it may perfect the always imperfect translation. It goes on, therefore, to infinity. But intuition, if intuition is possible, is a simple act" (Rugg 1963:209-210).

"There is," states Ortega y Gasset, "a broader use of the term 'reason' which includes everything that is not blind, everything that has <u>nous</u>

meaning" (Ortega 1960:189). Since behavior is implicitly meaningful, directed by a dynamic and teleological reality, it may well be, as Mach once suggested, that the purpose of all theory is merely to comprehend practice. (Polanyi 1958:145)

All knowledge is ultimately an outgrowth of commitment, of an emotional involvement with particular ends. In this sense, a specific commitment always entails a subsequent interpretation of the world. We question reality selectively, but even our questions tend to serve as hypothetical answers in the sense that our questions emerge from our goals, our goals from our values and so on. As Polanyi states, "...the person commits himself to certain beliefs and appreciations, and accepts certain meanings by deliberately merging his awareness of certain particulars into a local awareness of a whole" (Polanyi 1958:57).

Obsession with one's problem is in fact the mainspring of all inventive power. Asked by his pupils in jest what they should do to become "a Pavlov," the master answered in all seriousness: "Get up in the morning with your problem before you. Breakfast with it. Go to the laboratory with it. Eat your lunch with it. Keep it before you after dinner. Go to bed with it in your mind. Dream about it." It is this unremitting preoccupation with this problem that lends to genius its proverbial capacity for taking infinite pains. And the intensity of our preoccupation with a problem generates also our power for reorganizing our thoughts successfully, both during the hours of search and afterwards.

"The key to insight is the incomplete act "(Rugg 1963:309).

"Some integrating, organizing force must therefore be postulated; some power which, as Peter McKellar says, working like a giant magnet, selectively picking up iron from a heterogeneous scrap heap, gathers together only the mutually attractive fragments. I suggest that there is, in the nature of the act, a tendency of response that turns this miscellany into order" (Rugg 1963:73).

As Rugg sees it, creative insight is always contingent on three underlying factors:

"... first, utter concentration of attention on the goal, to the exclusion of outer and inner stimuli; second, continuous scanning or <u>searching movement of the total organism</u>, uninterruptedly <u>seeking completion</u>; third, completion (that is, 'flash of meaning') achieved when the adjustment of the organism to the demands of the situation has reached 'the canonical position,' to use McCulloch's terms, that is, when the group of space-time coordinates 'brings the object into identity with itself like rotations about an axis of symmetry,' as [W. Grey] Walter phrased it. The complete absorption in contemplation of the goal seems to pull together the needed elements into perfect fit" (Rugg 1963:309).

Intuitive thought is always directed by some vague foreknowledge--some intimation--of an ultimate goal or solution to the problem-at-hand. Thus, faced with a new situation, I respond pre-rationally in terms of subliminal movements. Such behavior-in-situation is the existential "meaning" of such a situation for me. My purpose in such a situation is, in essence, the fullest realization of my ongoing behavior.

My response will, then, be contingent on two underlying factors: (1) the objective nature of the situation as such, and (2) my subjective (motor-affective) responses to this situation. In all events, however, my behavior is mediated not by the situation <u>per se</u> but, rather, by my motor-affective response to such a situation.

My behavior will be determined primarily by my motor responses which have, in turn, been determined by the extent to which such responses have been experienced as effective (goal-satisfying) in the past. Since I can only respond in terms of what I already know how to do--that is, in terms of the repertoire of responses which is already available to me on the basis of the emotional consequences of my past experience--I find myself in the predicament of seeking the completion of acts which have already been substantially completed by prior practice and in terms of which certain terminal experiences (or consummations) have already been achieved. Indeed, it is the fact that they have been experienced already that allows me to anticipate them (as a projected anticipation based upon memory) to be possible solutions to the problem at hand.

In a sense, then, faced with the same or similar situations, I will naturally seek the resolution of that behavior which is intuitively associated with such a situation. I will be guided in the course of my actions by serial goal-reductions on the basis of cues implicit within the cycle of behavior itself, behavior which will be guided by the motor-image of act-completions associated with similar actions in the past.

Ultimately, then, and as Polanyi so eloquently argues, it is useless to talk about <u>impersonal</u> knowledge, for the simple reason that all knowledge is fundamentally knowledge about behavior and not about "conditions" underlying behavior. As Polanyi writes:

"Formalization can be carried beyond this point, but only for an 'object theory' described within a meta-theory which is itself informal" (Polanyi 1958:258).

Kleene states, "An intuitive mathematics is necessary even to define the formal mathematics" (Kleene 1951:62).

We may try to supply this criterion by defining mathematics as the totality of theorems derived from a certain set of axioms according to certain operations which will assure their self-consistency, provided the axioms themselves are mutually consistent. But this is still inadequate. First, because it leaves completely unaccounted for the choice of axioms, which hence must appear arbitrary--which it is not; second, because not all mathematics considered to be well established has ever been completely formalized according to strict procedure; and third, because--as K. R. Popper has pointed out--among the propositions that can be derived from some accepted set of axioms there are still, for every single one that represents a significant mathematical theorem, an infinite number that are trivial.

All these difficulties are but consequences of our refusal to see that mathematics cannot be defined without acknowledging its most obvious feature: namely, that it is interesting (Polanyi 1958:187-188).

Mathematics aside, however, and as Karl Marx once stated: "...the reason is not to be found in <u>consciousness</u>, but in <u>being</u>; not in thinking, but in living; it is to be found in the empirical development and self-expression of the individual, which, in turn, depends on the conditions of the world in which he lives" (Fromm 1962:114).

Intuitive thought is expressed by means of subliminal motor responses and directed by means of incipient motor relationships. Contemporary evidence suggests that these motor responses probably correspond to some sort of dynamic isomorphic structure in the nervous system in which electro-chemical traces of past stimuli persevere in some system of dynamic configuration within the brain. Such pre-established patterns of meaning, emerging out of past experience and therefore out of prior behavior, are reactivated in the process of ongoing behavior and serve to direct such behavior. As philosopher Alan Watts writes, in describing such a process:

"The human behavior that we call perception, thought, speech, and action is a consistency of organism and environment of the same kind as eating. What happens when we touch and feel a rock? Speaking very crudely, the rock comes in touch with a multitude of nerve ends in our fingers, and any nerve in the whole pattern of ends which touches the rock 'lights up.' Imagine that enormous grid of electric light bulbs connected with a tightly packed grid of push buttons. If I open my hand and with its whole surface push down a group of buttons, the bulbs will light up in a pattern approximately resembling my hand. The shape of the hand is 'translated' into the pattern of buttons and bulbs. Similarly, the feeling of a rock is what happens to the grid of the nervous system when it translates a contact with the rock.

But we have at our disposal 'grids' far more, complex than this--not only optical and auditory but also linguistic and mathematical. These, too, are patterns into whose terms the world is translated into nerve patterns. Such a grid, for example, is the system of coordinates, three of space and one of time, in which we feel that the world is happening even though there is no actual line of height, width, and depth filling all space, and though the earth does not go <u>tick-tock</u> when it revolves. Such a grid is also the whole system of classes, or verbal pigeon-holes, into which we sort the world as things or events; still or moving; light or dark; animal, vegetable, or mineral; bird, beast, or flower; past, present, or future" (Watts 1961:30-31).

In a sense, of course, the entire process is very similar to what occurs in analogical computers which have been programmed to recognize and respond in certain ways to preformulated patterns of coded stimuli. The neurological "grid"-system serves as a filter between sensation and perception. As cyberneticist Norbert Wiener states:

"What is important is not merely the information that we put into the line, but what is left of it when it goes through the final machinery to open or close sluices, to synchronize generators, and to do similar tasks. In one sense, this terminal apparatus may be regarded as a filter superimposed on the transmission line. Semantically significant information from the cybernetic point of view is that which gets through the line-plus-filter, rather than that which gets through the line alone. In other words, when I hear a passage of music, the greater part of the sound gets to my sense organs and reaches my brain. However, if I lack perception and training necessary for the aesthetic understanding of musical structure, this information will meet a block, whereas if I were a trained musician it would meet an interpreting structure or organization which would exhibit the pattern in a significant form which can lead to aesthetic appreciation and further understanding. Semantically significant information in the machine as well as in man is information which gets through to an activating mechanism in the system that receives it, despite man's and/or nature's attempts to subvert it" (Wiener 94).

What sets the human computer apart from the non-human variety is its capacity for "flexible scheduling"--its capacity to monitor its own feedback and to reprogram itself creatively on the basis of an esthetic feeling aimed at bringing esthetic closure in the direction of its own pervasive purposes. Machines can be programmed to be purposive, and such "purposeful behavior" can be made both sustaining and self-modifying. Initially, however--to this point in time--a machine must be programmed by human intelligence. Unlike human beings, machines do not yet behave spontaneously and learn from their own spontaneously generated activities. Perhaps even more basic--even in those cases where energy, motility, sentiency and so on are artificially supplied--machines lack the spontaneous inclination to transform their own experiences symbolically, to derive their own symbolic apparatus for self-instruction. They can--as yet--symbolize only formally (logically) in terms of human codifications of experience. (The increasing interest in programming computers to perform what is generally termed "fuzzy logic" is actually based on the notion that human thought is fundamentally a process of "approximation and correction" that calls for a constant matching and modifying of concepts in order to align and prioritize the most effective conceptual responses to anticipated problems.)

At basis, then, the motor-affective processes are interrelated with latent neurological processes which serve to direct and organize subsequent perceptual experience. Existing neurological patterns correspond to previously established patterns of experienced behavior. In successful intuition, and as Watts so accurately observes, "the regularities of nature are the regularities of our grids," (Watts 1961:31) and our tendencies to respond correspond to the sort of behavior which is objectively necessitated by the instrumental requirements of the situation-at-hand. In unsuccessful intuition we seek to impose our conditioned proclivities to respond upon circumstances which demand a different sort of behavior altogether--something radically at odds with what occurs in self-actualizing cognition.

In a sense, of course, an intuitive response to the total meaning of a situation is a skill, consisting of latent sequences of specific behaviors, and not a <u>knowledge</u> in the usual sense at all. As a skill, it is not ordinarily restricted to specific situations or specific content but can be expressed through different media and through the utilization of different senses and different parts of the body, providing that the "meaning"--that is, the implicitly purposive sequence of interwoven motor-affective responses leading to a sense of esthetic closure--is neither blocked nor interrupted.

At basis, then, intuitive thought functions as subliminal cue-reintegration by means of serial motor-responses. Each motor-response, if effective, (1) confirms the heuristic nature of the preceding response and (2) serves as the stimulus for directing and organizing the next. Each effective response within a sequence also serves to intensify motivation toward the implicit goal of heightening proximity to reward (in what is termed the <u>goal-gradient effect</u>) and, hence, further directs and intensifies activities with respect to the ultimate goal.

Intuitive thought is, then, basically an organized association (or patterning) of instrumental relationships which are "felt" (motor-affectively) to cohere within themselves and to be congruent within some more encompassing action-orientation. It implies, not particular acts, but, rather, particular relationships of acts with respect to some nonverbal goal. The same pattern of relationships can be expressed through different modes of activity--the same rhythm can be created on a drum or with a flute, the same idea may be represented graphically or verbally, by dance, picture or written word.

The fact that equivalent meanings can be projected into objectively different situations can be demonstrated by the so-called "perceptual constancies"- brightness constancy, size constancy, shape constancy, and so on. In each case, and as Berelson indicates, "...not only the specific object but the others surrounding it vary accordingly, so that the <u>relationship</u> between them remains constant. The black suit as well as the white shirt reflects less light at night: the luminosity relationship, and thus perceived whiteness, remains constant"(Berelson 117-118).

The point is, of course, that we see white shirts at night as <u>white</u> and not as the gray they might otherwise appear to be precisely because we are capable of transposing the meaning of sense-presentations on the basis of certain constant relationships which take precedence over, and become determinative of, the contingent nature of particular circumstances.

The intuitive process itself is directed in three ways: conatively, normatively and "cognitively." In a sense, the process begins with conation with an experienced tendency toward some type of activity which is not consciously identified. Such activity initiates behavior and serves to define the general area of interest or involvement. As Polanyi indicates:

"The decisive part which intellectual passions have been shown to play in the several domains of natural science, engineering, and mathematics, demonstrates the ubiquity of such [conative] participation. In each of these domains it is the relevant intellectual passion which affirms the distinctive intellectual values by which any particular performance may qualify for admittance to the domain. The arts appear then no longer as contrasted but as immediately continuous with science, only that in them the thinker participates more deeply in the object of his thought" (Polanyi 1958:194).

Conation, however, merely initiates and sustains activity. The channelization and interpretation of such behavior is contingent upon the more developed cognitive and normative processes--particularly the classification of goals in terms of more abstract values. Through normification, conative behavior becomes defined conceptually in terms of actual objects or objectives: interests become construed in terms of actual object referents. But, once the initial conative and normative aspects of behavior have occurred, the stage is set for the "cognitive," or problem-solving, component of intuitive behavior.

This phase ordinarily evolves through three stages: (1) problem-perceiving, (2) the intuitive definition of the solution, and (3) the practical testing of the solution in terms of behavioral consequences.

Problem-perception

Problem-perception occurs when there is a disruption in otherwise spontaneous instrumental behavior--where, in short, a sequence of ongoing (conative) activity (which may or may not be directed toward some conscious, normative, end) is blocked by some perceived difficulty. In a sense, of course, problem-perception is itself contingent upon a redirection of attention (or conation) toward some encountered difficulty and the subsequent (normative) labeling of the difficulty as a disvalue with respect to some encountered situation. This is followed by a temporary rechanneling of volition away from the ultimate goal and toward the proximate goal of doing away with the presented problem as a way of returning to the main course of action. In this sense, all problem-perception necessarily occurs only within a more encompassing (and frequently tacit) problem-orientation which acts as the ultimate source of intellectual orientation.

The Intuitive Definition of the Solution

The intuitive definition of the solution encompasses three inextricably related steps:

1) There is a tacit conviction--a "physical certainty"--that the problem is soluble; a conviction which is, in all likelihood, conditioned primarily upon (a) the strength of the motivating drive itself and (b) the individual's past success in solving the same or similar sorts of problems;

2) There is an intuitive definition of the solution itself which encompasses two dialectical dimensions of problem-solving: the internal and the external;

3) There is the selection of a preferred solution to the problem-at-hand.

1) <u>The Conviction of Solubility.</u> In a sense, of course, the conviction that the problem is amenable to solution is implicit in the recognition of the <u>problem</u> as a problem in the first place. A problem is, after all, and as Kurt Lewin, has remarked, a "quasi-need" which derives from goal-seeking behavior and which therefore functions as a sort of secondary value. At basis, then, and as Polanyi states, the problem "arrives accredited in advance by the heuristic craving which evoked it" (Polanyi 1958:130). As he states:

"... a problem is the intimation of a hidden rational relationship which is felt to be accessible by a heuristic effort, and the discovery of which may be accompanied, even in animals, by the lively enjoyment of their own ingenuity" (Polanyi 1958:366-7).

In a sense, of course, the solution of any problem is implicit within (1) the subjective (instrumental) nature of the problem as perceived and (2) the objective (logical) organization of conditions within the problem-situation. To merely perceive a problem is, in a sense, to initiate behavior with respect to it. Such behavior is purposive and seeks its completion in the realization of its own goal, the solution of the problem.

In pure intuition, the solution of the problem is perceived not as a hypothetical solution, but, rather, as the step by step emergence of each component act within the ideo-motor process itself. Once the sequence of problem-solving behavior has been initiated, each act implies, by preverbal motor-association--by "feeling" or "fitness"--what the succeeding act will be. The completed sequence of acts, in turn, gradually assumes a visible form, or organization, which inclines itself, by means of its own tacit logic toward a solution. As Polanyi states:

"Though the solution of a problem is something we have never met before, yet in the heuristic process it plays a part similar to the mislaid fountain pen or the forgotten name which we know quite well. We are looking for it as if it were there, pre-existent. Problems set to students are of course known to have a solution; but the belief that there exists a hidden solution which we may be able to find is essential also in envisaging and working at a never yet solved problem. It determines also the manner in which the 'happy thought' eventually presents itself as something inherently satisfying. It is not one among a great many ideas to be pondered upon at leisure, but one which carries conviction from the start.... this is a necessary consequence of the way a heuristic striving evokes its own consummation" (Polanyi 1958:126-7).

This same process applies to scientific problem-solving where any process of enquiry unguided by intellectual passions would inevitably spread out into a desert of trivialities. Our vision of reality, to which our sense of scientific beauty responds, must suggest to us the kind of questions that it should be reasonable and interesting to explore. It should recommend the kind of conceptions and empirical relations that are intrinsically plausible and which should therefore be upheld, even when some evidence seems to contradict them, and tell us also, on the other hand, what empirical connections to reject as specious, even though there is evidence for them--evidence that we may as yet be unable to account for on any other assumptions. In fact, without a scale of interest and plausibility based on a vision of reality, nothing can be discovered that is of value to science; and only our grasp of scientific beauty, responding to the evidence of our senses, can evoke this vision (Polanyi 1958:135).

Phrased somewhat differently, the existence of a problem ordinarily implies the existence of a solution. This is true for a number of reasons, but, perhaps most significantly, because, since meaning is inextricably wed to cause-and-effect determinism, it stands to reason that all problems are soluble (at least in principle) if they are comprehensible--that is, "make sense"--in the first place. This is true, because being soluble (explicable) is one of the qualifications for being termed comprehensible. In this sense, and as philosopher John Hospers indicates:

"There is even a sense in which a square circle is conceivable: namely that the words in the expression "square circle," though they contradict each other, have a definite cognitive meaning. If they did not, you could not know what it designates is logically impossible. In this rather strange sense, a square circle is conceivable, but a glaminated sirophent is not, because, 'glaminated sirophent' is a (cognitively) meaningless expression, designating nothing logically possible <u>or</u> impossible" (Hospers 1953:98).

In addition, of course, problems are relative to values, and, since values tend to be self-confirming, they tend to engender a continuing interest in a generically similar set of problems which are amenable to solution by means of already established patterns of problem-solving behavior.

As Polanyi indicates, it may be that, contrary to popular opinion, science not only makes metaphysical assumptions of an absolutistic nature but that these assumptions act heuristically to engender a firm conviction with respect to the ultimate rationality of nature itself. Again, to quote Polanyi:

"... personal knowledge in science is not made but discovered, but as such it claims to establish contact with reality beyond the clues on which it relies. It commits us, passionately and far beyond our comprehension into a vision of reality.... I called it the discovery of rationality in nature, a name which was meant to say that the kind of order which the discoverer claims to see in nature goes far beyond his understanding; so that his triumph lies precisely in his foreknowledge of a host of yet hidden implications which his discovery will reveal in later days to other eyes" (Polanyi 1958:64).

2) <u>The Intuitive Definition of the Solution</u>. There is an intuitive definition of the solution itself. This encompasses two dialectical dimensions of problem-solving the <u>internal</u> and <u>external.</u>

The <u>internal</u> dialectic is implied by the nature of the ongoing behavior itself. It encompasses all of that behavior which is necessitated by the inherent logic of the act.

All behavior, conscious or otherwise, is directed by its own inherent logic. As Polanyi indicates, there is even a sort of "inarticulate logic of animals" (Polanyi 1958:184) which is dictated by the comprehension of certain conditions (and therefore objectively necessitated regularities) within experience itself. Behavior is not <u>causa sui</u>. It emerges in terms of ordered tendencies and preformed response-patterns which <u>indirectly</u> reflect the objective structure of underlying reality.

"The logical premises of factuality are not known to us or believed by us <u>before</u> we start establishing facts, but are recognized on the contrary <u>by reflecting on the way we establish facts</u>... We do not believe in the existence of facts because of our anterior and secure belief in any explicit logical presuppositions of such a belief; but on the contrary, we believe in certain explicit presuppositions of factuality only because we have discovered that they are implied in our belief in the existence of facts" (Polanyi 1958:162).

In a sense, then, the psychological (subjective) inclinations of the individual inevitably emerge out of a personal awareness of the logical (objective) possibilities which inhere within reality itself and which are comprehended on the basis of prior practical behavior.

In the final analysis, the old dichotomy between the <u>logical</u> and the <u>psychological</u> is a bogus one. Psychological (subjective), behavior is always the outgrowth of formative logical (objective) behavior which occurred prior to, and which is therefore determinative of, the development of the ego itself. In a phenomenological sense, there is always a logic to behavior, and even ostensibly "illogical" behavior is necessarily conditioned by the nature of objective (behavioral) conditions which have been experienced in the past.

The laws of logic are the laws implicit within reality itself. Reality is knowable only through behavior. Behavior is invariably instrumental and goal-directed. Logic is then one way in which we describe the laws which govern effective behavior, and the principles of logic are inseparable from a formal explication of effective practice at the highest level of abstraction.

Phrased somewhat differently, the laws of logic are not only <u>truths</u> but <u>values</u> as well, because logic is a psychological necessity both for survival and for success within survival. <u>Psychological</u> errors (as Socrates recognized) are invariably <u>logical</u> errors as well, for the psychological processes are invariably conditioned by objective (logical) necessity, and such principles are sustained, not only by the earliest pre-reflective behavior, but by subsequent demands for effective practice in the course of everyday experience.

To act intuitively--unreflectively--is not, then, to act illogically but, quite the contrary, to act in terms of the pre-established "behavioral logic" implied by the objective circumstances at hand. In a sense, the solution of the problem emerges out of the behavioral response to the problem, and it may be described as a "dawning awareness" of the meaning and significance implicit within one's own spontaneous actions. Such an insight is largely an awareness of the logic and the logical implications of one's own personal behavior. As Polanyi notes with reference to mathematics:

"The manner in which the mathematician works his way towards discovery, by shifting his confidence from intuition to computation and back again from computation to intuition, while never releasing his hold on either of the two, represents in miniature the whole range of operations by which articulation disciplines and expands the reasoning powers of man. This alternation is asymmetrical, for a formal step can be valid only by virtue of our tacit confirmation of it. Moreover, a symbolic formalism is itself but an embodiment of our antecedent unformalized powers--an instrument skillfully contrived by our inarticulate selves for the purpose of relying on it as our external guide. The interpretation of primitive terms and axioms is therefore predominantly inarticulate, and so is the process of their expansion and re-interpretation which underlies the progress of mathematics. The alternation between the intuitive and the formal depends on tacit affirmations, both at the beginning and at the end of each chain of formal reasoning" (Polanyi 1958:131).

The <u>external</u> (or informal) dialectic is that which is implied by the relationship between past experience and present experience. It encompasses all of that behavior which is necessitated by the relatively fortuitous association of past experience--expressed in terms of both knowledge and values--which is brought to bear upon the present problem- situation. These relationships are governed less by logical implication than by psychological (conative) associations which are controlled by factors with in the organism itself.

3) <u>Selection to the Preferred Solution</u>. There is the selection to the preferred solution to the problem-at-hand.

Hypotheses, or tentative solutions, with respect to the problem-at-hand are derived either from the internal dialectic by means of purely formal inference on the basis of pre-existing knowledge, or from the external dialectic, on the basis of informal (psychological) and more or less "creative" conjecture on the basis of the perceived relationship between past and present experience as these relate to existing needs and goals.

With respect to the hypothesizing process, there are two basic types of intuitive thought: (1) <u>pure intuition</u> in which behavior is direct and unmediated by conscious ideation of the usual symbolic sort, and (2) what might be termed <u>"mixed" intuition</u>, in which behavior is mediated by some sort of "informed insight."

In the latter case, it is important to distinguish between "intuition" <u>per se</u> which is always, as Bruner states, "the intellectual technique of arriving at plausible but tentative formulations without going through the analytic steps by which such formulations would be found to be valid or invalid conclusions," (Bruner 13) and "insight," which--however intuitive it may have been in its origins--always consists of some degree of conscious knowledge which is used for empirical guidance.

All intuition, however "pure" in derivation it may be, normally gives rise to some sort of knowledge by means of cognitive feedback and is therefore a potential source of insight as well. In a sense, of course, the distinction between <u>intuition</u> and <u>insight</u> might be summarized by saying that <u>intuition</u> is basically a skill, or <u>knowing how</u>, while <u>insight</u> is fundamentally a belief, or <u>knowing that</u>.

As discussed, all intuition is directed by some process of anticipated solution. In pure intuition, however, these solutions remain tacit and inhere within the motor behavior itself. Whether tacit or explicit, however, all thought necessarily advances by intuitive conjecture which is based on the application of either pre-existing patterns of behavior or prior knowledge that relate to the solution of existing problems.

Both formal and informal thought are equally dependent upon the intuitive process in which knowledge that grows out of past experience is related to the solution of present problems. In a sense, then, all hypothesizing is necessarily intuitive and therefore creative, because it acts as the relationing of behavior which is objectively (necessarily) dissociated until it is connected on the basis of personal experience (which is always selective and goal- seeking in nature).

At basis, all hypotheses--all project solutions--are either directly or indirectly the product of volitional activity which necessarily precedes any sort of verification, and all hypotheses are necessarily good or bad, correct or incorrect, <u>after the fact</u> on the basis of their experienced consequences in actual behavior. <u>A good, or effective, hypothesis is, in effect, an hypothesis which is advanced psychologically (behaviorally) but which subsequently proves to satisfy the logical (objective) requirements of the situation-at-hand.</u> This is not, of course, to say that effective experience is purely contingent on good hypotheses relative to existing problems. Obviously, many other factors must be taken into consideration. A good informal (creative) hypothesis may, for example, be applied illogically or improperly. Perhaps even more basic, good hypotheses may be applied to the solution of bad, unreal or insignificant, problems and may, in this sense, be "productive" only in a very qualified sense of the word.

Thought as Holistic

Thinking occurs through an established hierarchy of meaning in which a higher, or more encompassing, knowledge of the total relationship necessarily assumes priority in the determination of more specific meanings.

Focal awareness, which gives rise to explicit knowledge, always stems from a more encompassing subsidiary awareness of the nature of the total behavioral pattern (which necessarily remains implicit). "Meaning perception"--to use Whitehead's term-- always precedes any "immediacy perception" of the component aspects within the overall conative-motor sequence of activity. In other words, object-perception--the interpretation of particulars--is always contingent upon a latent awareness of some meaningful context which includes some sense of governing intent.

In one of the better-known experiments conducted by Ames and his associates over a generation ago, a rubber ball was propped against a featureless backdrop and inflated. It was discovered that such a ball was perceived by experimental subjects to retain its initial size and to be drawing nearer. In short, since balls do not ordinarily inflate themselves spontaneously, the inflation of the ball was interpreted as movement toward the subject despite oculo-motor cues of a purely physical sort which would have normally suggested a different conclusion altogether (Polanyi 1958:96).

As the Ames laboratory experiments indicate, perception is invariably a comprehension of clues in terms of some pre-established sense of general meaning. Ultimately, and as philosopher Benedetto Croce has said, physical facts as such "do not possess reality" (Croce 154). Rather, and as Polanyi indicates, knowing is

"...an active comprehension of the things known, an action that requires skill. Skillful knowing and doing is performed by subordinating a set of particulars, as clues or tools, to the shaping of a skillful achievement, whether practical or theoretical. We may then be said to become 'subsidiarily aware' of these particulars within our 'focal awareness' of the coherent entity that we achieve. Clues and tools are things used as such and not observed in themselves" (Polanyi 1958:vii).

A subsidiary awareness of the total pattern of ongoing behavior serves both to encompass and to direct local awareness. We are subsidiarily aware of those things that we "know" but disregard.

In a sense, we <u>attend through</u> our subsidiary awareness in order to specific content. As Polanyi indicates:

"When we use a hammer to drive in a nail, we attend to both nail and hammer, <u>but in a different way</u>. We <u>watch</u> the effect of our strokes on the nail and try to wield the hammer so as to hit the nail most effectively. When we bring down the hammer we do not feel that its handle has struck our palm but that its head has struck the nail. Yet, in a sense we are certainly alert to the feelings in our palm and the fingers that hold the hammer. They guide us in handling it effectively, and the degree of attention that we give to the nail is given to the same extent but in a different way to these feelings. The difference may be staled by saying that the latter are not, like the nail, objects of our attention, but instruments of it. They are not watched in themselves; we watch something else while keeping intensely aware of them. I have a <u>subsidiary awareness</u> of the feeling in the palm of my hand which is merged into my <u>focal awareness</u> of my driving in the nail" (Polanyi 1958:55).

In a similar sense he writes,

"While we rely on a tool or a probe, these are not handled as external objects. We may test the tool for its effectiveness or the probe for its suitability, e.g., in discovering the hidden details of a cavity, but the tool and the probe can never lie in the field of these operations;, they remain necessarily on our side of it, forming part of ourselves, the operating person. We pour ourselves into them and assimilate them as parts of our own existence. We accept them existentially by dwelling in them" (Polanyi 1958:59).

The behavioral-Gestalt is, then, apprehended by means of continual "sensory-motor awareness." Like unphotographed scenery, it is not "recorded" but, rather, "undergone."

Subsidiary experience can never become focal experience--"knowledge" in the usual sense of the term--without changing its nature as subsidiary experience. To focus on the whole is momentarily to change the whole to part, just as, in a similar sense, to focus on some aspect of what was previously focal knowledge is to transform the prior locus into subsidiary awareness. Again, and as Polanyi notes:

"Subsidiary awareness and local awareness are mutually exclusive. If a pianist shifts his attention from the piece he is playing to the observation of what he is doing with his fingers while playing it, he gets confused and may have to stop. This happens generally if we switch our focal attention to particulars of which we have previously been aware only in their subsidiary role.

"The kind of clumsiness which is due to the fact that focal attention is directed to the subsidiary elements of an action is commonly known as self consciousness" (Polanyi 1958:56).

It is interesting to conjecture about the extent to which much focal cognition may actually be used as a "flight to reality"--that is, as a flight to verbal cognition--in the face of underlying intuitive anxiety. As psychologist Rollo May inquires:

"... is not the why asked so much in our culture precisely as a way of detaching ourselves, a way of avoiding the more disturbing and anxiety-creating alternative of sticking to the end with the what? This is not to say, the excessive preoccupation with causality and function that characterizes modern Western society may well serve, much more widely than realized, the need to abstract ourselves from the given reality of the given experience. Asking <u>why</u> is generally in the service of a need to get <u>over</u> the phenomenon, in line with Bacon's dictum, 'knowledge is power' and specifically, knowledge of nature is power over nature. Asking the question of <u>what</u>, on the other hand, is a way of <u>participating</u> in the phenomenon" (May 1967:83).

In a similar sense, and as Zen scholar Daisetz Suzuki indicates with respect to traditional psychoanalytic practice:

"It is characteristic of all true insight in psychoanalysis that it cannot be formulated in thought, while it is characteristic of all bad analysis that "insight" is formulated in complicated theories which have nothing to do with immediate experience. The authentic psychoanalytic insight is sudden; it arrives without being forced or even being premeditated. It starts not in our brain but, to use a Japanese image, in our belly. It cannot be adequately formulated in words and it eludes one if one tries to do so: yet it is real and conscious, and leaves the person who experiences it a changed person" (Suzuki 1956:32).

Subsidiary awareness is always purposive and instrumental in nature. What philosopher Frank Saunders terms the <u>qualitative pervasive</u> of felt-thought is not merely "emotional" in the usual sense of the word. In a far deeper sense, it is directive and unfolds as an esthetic imperative toward the full realization of some incipient act.

Intuition is, then, primarily expressive. It knows itself only by means of its own contingent particulars just as these particulars are known only within the expressive context of ongoing intuitive activity.

5. Pleasure/Pain/Happiness

The highest intrinsic good for any person is pleasure. It is the first (positive) psychological value that is experienced, and it remains the basic constituent in all subsequent positive psychological values that are learned later.

Any discussion of pleasure and pain is extremely complex and to become seriously engaged in such would go beyond the reasonable bounds of the present discussion. On the other hand, in a general sense, pleasure and pain are essentially elements involved in bringing life-forces into or out of equilibrium.

Pleasure is the psychological experience of electro-chemical processes in the central nervous system that are activated by the anticipated or experienced closure with respect to some ongoing, goal-oriented behavior. For all practical purposes, pleasure occurs when a problem is solved.

Frustration is the psychological experience engendered by the blocking or interference with some ongoing, goal-oriented behavior. Frustration occurs, for all practical purposes, when a problem becomes aggravated (or more problematic).

Pain is the psychological experience of electro-chemical processes in the central nervous system that are activated by the anticipated or experienced unsuccessful termination of some ongoing, goal-oriented behavior. It occurs when a problem is perceived to be insoluble. Physical pain as opposed to psychological pain is a subjective experience of genetically programmed electro-chemical processes in the central nervous system in response to actions that directly or indirectly threaten the survival or integrity of the physical organism itself and have therefore been genetically programmed through species-evolution.

For the sake of simplicity, I will tend to use the terms pleasure and pain, ignoring their logical contraries and opposites as well as the various emotional states, like anxiety, that are frequently associated with them.

The highest natural good on a psychological basis is happiness. Happiness is an abstract concept for a pattern of behavior that is designed to initiate, sustain and augment the optimum quantity and quality of pleasurable experience over the maximum period of time. Phrased somewhat differently, a concept of personal happiness is, in essence, a theory that purports to advance a synergistic cycle of pleasurable experience in which pleasurable behavior in one instance increases the probability or degree of pleasure in subsequent instances over the longest period of time.

Again, this is terribly over simplistic. Since a particular type of behavior may be directed by a variety of different motives--I may read a book for intellectual curiosity and also to pass an examination--and a variety of different behaviors may be underway at any one point in time--I may be doing brain surgery and earning a living concurrently--the nexus of behavior at any particular point in time is exceedingly complicated to pin down. Problem-solving is complicated. Problem-perception is even more complicated. Without the "aesthetic" orchestration provided by the intuitive processes that screen and sort competing response-sets on a pre-cognitive basis, the entire process would be virtually impossible to control.

Pleasure/Self-Actualization/Science/Society

Pleasure occurs when ongoing behavior leads to some kind of effective closure, but evidence in the case of virtually any kind of behavior, from murder to sado-masochism, is capable of yielding pleasure.

This means that self-actualization as a general concept is not applicable as a guide for behavior in general, because sometimes behavior is essentially self-defeating or dysfunctional in terms of creating or sustaining the sort of society that makes personal self-actualization possible or probable as a viable goal.

Science--which is a self-correcting process of inquiry that best approximates self-actualizing objectivity on a social scale--indicates that human behavior is directed toward five basic ends:

1) the satisfaction of biological needs:
2) the satisfaction of the needs for personal security;
3) the satisfaction of the needs to love and to be loved;
4) the satisfaction of ego-needs, the needs for personal recognition; and
5) the various needs for self-actualization.

These, listed in Maslow's rough sequence of developmental priority, are the basic human needs, but--unfortunately--all of these have logically contrary and opposite expressions which are just as capable of being realized as are the conventional "positive" expressions. If man has the capacity to love, he also has the capacity to hate (the opposite of love) or to be indifferent (which is its contrary).

A close examination, however, reveals that there are particular expressions of each category of behavior that provide a basis for the next level of need in the sequence and which, moreover, provide an element of what can constitute a total and interlocking pattern of relationships that sustains and advances positive self-actualizing societies while, at the same time, promoting what is, in essence, a society that guarantees the possibility of self-actualization for all of its members. Thus, in such a society

a) Biological needs imply a society that is characterized by prosperity and an equitable distribution of basic material requirements for all.
b) Security needs imply a society at peace with other nations and enjoying domestic tranquility at home.
c) The need for love implies a social ethic approximating the Golden Rule and a generally altruistic orientation toward others.
d) The need for individual recognition implies a society which allows each person the freedom to express his own differences and to be valued for such differences provided that they are compatible with the conditions required for universal self-actualization for all.
e) The need for self-actualization as such suggests a society that provides the ability (education) and opportunity (leisure) for a person to fully develop his own intellectual, aesthetic and creative needs to the maximum degree possible.

Such a society would provide the maximum correlation between inclination and opportunity. In such a society each individual would have the ability to be self-actualizing, providing only that he act in such a way as to preserve and promote the self-actualization of others as well. The result would be a circular process of positive synergism. The society promotes the self-actualization of the individual, and each individual self-actualizer promotes the social conditions that advance his own self-actualization.

The Intellectual Bases of Ethics
Philosophy
    (gives rise to)
Science
    (which gives rise to)
Scientific psychology
    (which, by means of clinical psychology, gives rise to)
Philosophical psychology (including self-actualization theory)

(which encourages)

Normative science (including clinical psychology)

   (which gives rise to)

Scientific ethics

   (which basically defines)

Social ethics

   (which finds its practical application in)

Political philosophy (which is applied ethics).

Deficiency Motivation and Frustration-Induced Learning

One of the most interesting features of coerced conversion is the similarity which it bears to what has been termed "frustration-induced learning," a term initially coined by psychologist Norman R F. Maier (Maier 1961:25) to describe certain types of behavior which he observed in a series of experiments concerned with card-discrimination learning in rats. In one series of these experiments Maier designed a problem in which laboratory rats were compelled to jump from a small platform across an intervening space to one of two cards, one marked with a white circle and one with a black circle, which blocked their access to food. If the rat leaped to the correct card, the card gave way and the rat was rewarded by being allowed access to the food on the platform. If it jumped to the wrong card, the card would fail to give way, and the rat would bump its nose and fall into a protective net suspended beneath the apparatus.

In what was ostensibly a standard card-discrimination problem, however, Maier introduced one very significant variation. He structured the learning situation in such a way that the food (reward) was placed at random order behind <u>either</u> of the cards <u>on each successive trial</u>. The problem was then, in essence, beyond solution since each card was unpredictably rewarding only half of the time. To break the rat's understandable resistance to jumping under such conditions a negative stimulus (a hissing jet of air) was used to compel the rats to leap from the platform to one or the other of the two cards.

The rats were, then, faced with a rather severe conflict situation in which no "good" or predominantly satisfying response was possible, but in which all escape was blocked and in which some kind of response was required by virtue of the circumstances at hand.

The results, as observed by Maier and subsequently corroborated by various other researchers as well, are extremely interesting. What Maier discovered was that the rats not only made choices but that the choices made characteristically evolved into an "abnormal fixation" on one of the two cards presented (Maier 1961:25). After several trials the rats would fixate on one of the two cards (usually on a situational basis, right or left) and would then consistently jump to the preferred card without deviation and <u>regardless</u> of subsequent rewards or punishments. Such behavior Maier has termed "frustration-induced." It differs from the usual sort of "motivation-induced" learning in five basic respects (Maier 1960).

1) Unlike the usual sort of "motivation-induced" learning, frustration-induced learning is not geared to the realization of some defined and recognizable goal. It is not "motivated" behavior in the usual sense of the word.[80]

2) It is stereotyped and rigid, even ritualistic. Frustration-induced learning is inflexible and nonadaptable. It may change in intensity but not in how it is expressed.

3) It is compulsive. Frustration-induced learning, once developed, is nonvolitional and functions independent of the original circumstances from which it was derived.

(The compulsive nature of frustration-induced learning can also be seen in the so called "dynamic stereotype" in the behavior of dogs which Pavlov observed occasionally to accompany certain extreme reactions to stress. Pavlov took the position that the severe excitation of one specific area of the dog brain could lead to a severe inhibition of response in other areas, a condition which would predispose toward compulsive repetitions in behavior.)

4) It is nonconstructive and/or destructive in nature. Frustration-induced learning does not, by virtue of its noninstrumental character, contribute to the effectiveness of future behavior. It is basically expressive-consummatory in nature and is nonadaptive in the usual sense.

It could be argued, of course--at least in the experiment described--that the rats behavior <u>was</u> actually the best response available. The problem was insoluble in nature, and it is hard to conceive of any response which could have been <u>more rational</u> or <u>more gratifying</u> than a stereotyped and compulsive one designed to yield the highest proportion of reward available under the circumstances. In most situations, the alternatives are scarcely so neat and well-balanced, and the consequences of fleeing to ritualistic behavior as a means of escaping the usual sort of problem-solving confrontation is ordinarily less fortunate.

In general, then, in frustration-induced learning the development of more effective behavior is blocked, and subsequent behavior tends to become fixated at, or even to regress back to, more primitive levels of response. In effect, a pattern of circular frustration is instituted. The behavioral dilemma with which the individual is faced creates stress which leads to a dysfunctional pattern of frustration-induced behavior. The frustration-induced response, while it may diminish stress in an <u>immediate</u> sense by providing an active release for existing tensions, serves to generate even more stress in the long run by perpetuating the original conflict situation and by generating additional punishments which create additional stress as well.

In a sense, then, frustration-induced behavior is reinforced in two ways. It is reinforced in an immediate sense by providing an outlet for contemporary tensions which is experienced as pleasurable. It is reinforced in a more long-term way by sustaining and even augmenting the very conditions necessary for its own survival. It generates precisely the kind of ultimate failure which is required to guarantee a repetition of those frustrations which are necessary to elicit its own subsequent recurrence.

5) It is aggravated by punishment. A frustration-induced response, once established, is extremely difficult to eliminate. As Maier indicates, even when a rat has developed a frustration-induced response to jump to one card, he will refuse food even when visible if it requires jumping to the "wrong" card or to the "wrong" side of the platform. In the case of frustration-induced learning, then, it is not enough that a solution be <u>available</u>. It must be <u>perceived</u>, and this is precisely what frustration-induced learning tends to preclude. The rat has one characteristic in common with the alcoholic, the bed-wetter and the thumb-sucker. They all respond <u>superstitiously</u>. Faced with a real problem for which they have no answer, they are compelled to act "without reason" since the consequences of doing nothing are significantly worse than the consequences of doing something (regardless of what this something may be), they are forced to respond. Since they have no answer to the <u>real</u> problem at hand, the problem must be implicitly redefined. In most cases, it evolves into a problem of what to do to relieve tension in the face of insupportable stress. The response which emerges under such conditions may be inappropriate, but it is nevertheless a type of "solution." It may not be the <u>best</u> answer to the problem, but it is a way of responding to a stressful situation in which the "problem" itself is largely problematic. In a sense, then, the answer to absurdity is the creation of gratuitous meaning, a sort of <u>ad lib</u> psychological structuring. Such structuring may not resolve the conflict but, in a sense, it allows such conflict to be expressed and, in so doing, it provides a real release for insupportable tension.

With regard to the first basic difference identified above--which holds that frustration-induced learning is not "motivated" behavior in the usual sense of the word--it seems safe to assume that Maier would take the position that even frustration-induced learning is "motivated" by a pervasive need to reduce tensions. What he seems to mean is that it is not "motivated" in the sense of being instrumental to the realization of some other <u>particular</u> end. Interestingly enough, Maslow seems to take much the same position with regard to the "unmotivated" behavior of the totally "self-actualizing person," who exists at the opposite end of the adjustmental continuum from the chronically frustrated.

In a sense, of course, it is true that the cessation of punishment creates a sense of positive affect and therefore serves as a source of pleasure (reward). In this respect, all punishments--except where artificially sustained and eventuating in the death of the organism--terminate in reward and, in a similar sense, the cessation of all rewards is experienced as punishment. In a more profound sense, what Maier's studies suggest are that there are three ways in which behavior may be controlled through reinforcement. These are (1) directly, by using rewards and punishments; (2) directly, by using rewards and refraining from the direct use of punishment; or (3) indirectly, by using punishments and refraining from the use of rewards.

The latter is what Maier describes in his experiments with the rats, and it is what frequently occurs in the earlier stages of the confession process in thought reform. This indirect method of controlling behavior through punishment can occur, of course, in either a <u>controlled</u> or <u>uncontrolled</u> setting. In an uncontrolled situation--as, for example, in a typical public high school--it is very difficult to determine what the consequences of punishments will be, because the student is confronted with a situation in which he is free to choose his own response (within very general limits) on the basis of his personal inclinations (values). The boy who has failed every examination or suffered a sufficient number of indignities at the hands of his teachers may, for example, drop out of school, study harder, or involve himself in any of a number of other possibilities on the basis of both personal and situational variables. In the totally controlled environment of thought reform, this does not occur because no "choice" as such is called for. The punishments are not used to <u>elicit decisions</u> but rather to

<u>compel behavior</u>. Such behavior is predefined, reinforced and sustained over a sufficient period of time to guarantee that it will be psychologically assimilated as a value. When this occurs, it becomes a basis for subsequent choices in uncontrolled situations as well (Maier 1960:24).

What must be recognized is that frustration-induced learning, while it may be nonconstructive or even destructive in a long-term sense, is both adaptive and constructive from the immediate and subjective point of view of the individual who is acting. It is, for example, all very well that I know why my good friend Harry drinks to excess. I may even know what he should do about his problem. The fact remains, however, that Harry himself does not see his problems with such dispassionate objectivity, and he is not capable of resolving it in the same facile way that I may suggest. Harry must "live" his problem.

Let us say, for example, that Harry's problem stems from an unsuccessful marriage. He has discovered after many years that he is not happy with his wife, who is a shrew, and that he would like a divorce. Typically, however, he finds that he is ambivalent about the prospect of a divorce. Since he is a responsible person and a good father as well as a husband, he finds that, although he dislikes his wife intensely, he loves his children and would like to protect them from the unavoidable anguish of becoming involved in a divorce. He finds that he is, in effect, faced with a choice of comparative evils. Since he can find no decision which would be unequivocally "good," he begins to respond to his problem differently. Instead of dealing with his real problem, the question of divorce, he begins to focus more and more on the symptoms of his problem, the frustrations arising from his dilemma. He begins to drink as a way of escaping his difficulty, as a way of avoiding a difficult decision.

At basis, then, Harry senses, quite correctly, that whatever he decides to do of a "realistic nature" will be difficult and painful. By doing <u>something else instead</u>--by drinking--he does not turn his back on pleasure and seek pain. Quite the contrary; he gradually senses that his problem is one which precludes pleasure (a "happy solution") and which is simply too painful to contemplate. His response is not merely to do something else instead but to do something which will relieve the tensions of <u>not confronting</u> that which should have been done to begin with.

In a sense, of course, the pleasure which Harry derives from his drinking stems from the fact that his drinking minimizes the pain associated with his unresolved predicament. His life has become a sort of holding action in the face of chronic frustration. What is easy to overlook, however, is that, from his <u>own</u> point of view, he succeeds in his attempt to avoid failure. His drinking may not make him happy, but it is expedient in warding off the far more acute distress of his own more basic and unendurable dilemma.

If I were to encounter Harry after ten years of alcoholism with the news that his children are now grown up and happily married and that his shrewish wife has become a thoroughly lovable person--with the news, in short, that his original problem no longer exists--my chances of altering his behavior would still not be great, for I would be talking to a different man now and not the old Harry at all. Indeed, the old Harry was a man who <u>sought pleasure</u>. The new Harry is essentially a man who <u>avoids pain</u>. He is, in other words, a man whose entire perception of reality has been radically affected by an adjustment to frustration, an adjustment which has, by now, become a wholesale substitute-adjustment. The new Harry is a man who has not only lived with frustration, but who has, in a very real sense, made his peace with it and formed an adjustment within it.

Over an extended period of time, then, certain things have happened to Harry. Circular frustration has generated a cumulative and chronic sense of anxiety which has gradually become a virtually inalienable aspect of his basic identity. The world was bad. Drink has made it increasingly worse. The effects have been compounded. The world has become increasingly darker. Stress has been exaggerated by the consequences of <u>fleeing</u> from stress. Alcohol has become increasingly more necessary, more rewarding, as a way of coping with an inalienable sense of anxiety.

Harry has long since learned to perceive the world differently than it was when he first began to drink. His initial problem was an unsatisfactory marriage. It is <u>now</u> the unsatisfactory secondary adjustment which he has made as a way of avoiding any meaningful confrontation with his initial problem. Harry, in other words, is no longer a man faced with a marital problem. He is now, first and foremost, an alcoholic. Like the rat confronted with the cards, Harry's problem is no longer how to gain the reward but how to minimize and avoid the punishments.

It may no longer be of great importance to Harry what has happened to his family. His alcoholism has in a sense freed him from this problem by giving him a more compelling but, in many respects, a more manageable difficulty to deal with. He started out as a man with a marital problem who drank. He is now a substantially different person. He is now an alcoholic who has family difficulties. In a sense, then, his hierarchy of values has undergone a significant shift. His alcoholism now functions independent of its originating circumstances. It is still nurtured by stress, but the stress itself is now compounded by a myriad of other problems, including an overriding sense of guilt, which far outweighs the original bugaboo of a dreaded divorce.

Harry, like the convict who cannot adjust to life on the outside and who prefers to return to his cell, has become habituated to frustration and finds it difficult--and, in a very basic sense, "frustrating"--to return to a world unbounded by frustration and pain. It does no good to take away the cards and show the rat the food on the left-hand side, because the rat "knows" emotionally--his whole response apparatus tells him--that the food is on the right. In a similar sense, it does no good to show Harry a different world, one which can be confronted on a new and positive basis, because deep down, "in his bones," Harry knows that there is <u>no</u> such world or, if there is, that it simply won't work <u>for him</u>. He has become habituated to failure and acclimated to coping with frustration as a way of life.

There are, in general, two ways in which frustration-induced learning may be altered once it has become established. These are (1) by removing the frustration or (2) by restructuring the frustration in such a way as to encourage the development of a different sort of behavior. There are two ways in which it is possible to remove frustration as a way of encouraging the emergence of positive, or motivation-induced, learning. Perhaps the simplest way is, as Maier suggests, to treat the individual rather than the situation (Maier 1960:483). In such cases an attempt is made to remove the problem itself as a way of eliminating stress and allowing normal patterns of goal-oriented behavior to become reestablished and consolidated.

Typically, three basic steps are involved. First, the individual is removed from the stress situation, either by isolation or by eliminating stress within the situation itself. . Second, the individual is encouraged to develop new and more constructive patterns for confronting such a stress situation if and when it should recur. Third, the individual is reintroduced to his original problem, which has now been largely neutralized by means of insight and, psychological preparation, and is encouraged to utilize his new patterns of perception and his expanded repertoire of responses as a way of resolving the problem without resorting to frustration-induced "coping" mechanisms.

The other way in which stress may be reduced sufficiently to allow for effective positive reconditioning is through what might be termed "the decay of the original problem". In this case, the original stress situation is neither eliminated nor restructured but tends to lose its significance by being subordinated to the secondary adjustment which has attached itself to the original stress-response. In other words, and as philosopher Ernst Junger has said, there is a very real sense in which an adjustment to pain can become a new and even preferable <u>type of goal-orientation</u>. As so many of the studies which have been done of human behavior under conditions of extreme stress suggest, there is a sense in which any sort of behavioral "closure"--even a negative or neurotic one--is an "adjustment" and, as an adjustment, is experienced as pleasurable. Even a neurotic response is, in this sense, generally preferable to the anguish of continued indecision.

On the other hand, what is so frequently overlooked is that, once an adjustment has been established--and even if it is a "neurotic adjustment"--attention is often shifted away from the original problem and begins to focus on the adjustment process itself. In a very important sense, the problem is now no longer a matter of "what to do" but rather <u>how and when</u> to do "what one already does." For example, once a man has settled into alcoholism as a way of coping with chronic stress, his problem is no longer <u>whether</u> to drink. This is now a <u>given</u>. His problems are now, properly speaking, <u>when to drink, what to drink and with whom</u>. In short, the alcoholic, like the diabetic, learns to live with his condition. He experiences himself as an alcoholic and finds new sources of satisfaction within that established frame of reference which are not entirely unlike those developed by the diabetic or the victim of long-term leukemia who must also come to terms with their conditions.

During the Second World War many observers remarked upon the oddly "liberating" feeling associated with living in a Europe occupied by the Germans. In a very basic sense, the German invasion narrowed down the anguishing field of choice for many people. By eliminating many if not most of these possibilities, the Germans highlighted those which remained. By reducing the ambiguity associated with a chaotic overplentitude of options, they minimized ambivalence and made direct and meaningful action a far more potent alternative.

Perhaps the best example of the alleviation of stress by the decay or redefinition of the original problem is afforded by the existentialists. For the existentialists, the ultimate insight occurs when the world is perceived to be "absurd," without transcendent meaning of any sort. When the existentialist reaches this point, he has reached the nadir of hopelessness in "fear and trembling." On the other hand, as the existentialists are quick to observe, to be "hopeless" in this sense is not to be "without hope" but, rather, to learn to "hope" in a new and substantially different way--that is, within the defined context of purely finite experience. In other words, to learn that nothing has absolute meaning is, in a very basic sense, to learn that one's own problems are also meaningless and contingent upon the continued affirmation of personal experience. To affirm absurdity, then, is basically to transvaluate one's own particular values and problems and to seek pleasure in a world in which "non-pleasure" (meaninglessness, entailing a certain amount of metaphysical pain) is the encompassing norm. The secular existentialists, as Sartre would seem to suggest, are basically those individuals who have transcended their frustrations by accepting the necessity of terminal (metaphysical) frustration and by seeking a <u>positive</u> adjustment within such a <u>negative</u> situation.

In still another sense, it might very well be held that the therapeutic value of possessing an insight into absurdity is that, for many people, to affirm absurdity is to eliminate guilt-feelings based upon the presupposition of inexorable absolute standards of right and wrong. Whether absurdity is more threatening than guilt or vice versa depends, of course, upon the life-experience of the individual who chooses. The choice is basically between being innocent in a world without meaning or guilty in a world with meaning.

For most people, there are few things more anguishing than the inability to choose in a world which requires choice as a prerequisite for effective action. One of the advantages of the total institution is that it substantially reduces the stress of having to choose. There is, for example, something comforting about the routine of the prison camp. It can serve as an "externalized neurosis" and is capable of providing many people with a wholly objective and ritualistic defense against the anxiety associated with the usual sort of free and rational determination of behavior.

Cohen indicates that externalized (institutional) stress under prison camp conditions frequently tended to alleviate internalized stress stemming from guilt both by isolating the individual from hitherto anguishing choice-situations and also by providing him with the sort of punishment necessary to atone for his real or imaginary sins. Numerous observers have indicated that the incidents of neurotic and psychosomatic disorders seemed to decline very noticeably in the German concentration camps, and various reports would indicate that much the same sort of thing tended to occur during the stress of war, as during the London Blitz of 1940. This would, among other things, suggest that, at least with certain people, attempts to augment stress by minimizing autonomy and systematically intensifying physical anguish may actually misfire, merely creating a sense of freedom from oppressive responsibility and a paradoxical sense of purification by means of punishment.

The other basic way to alter frustration-induced learning is by restricting stress in such a way as to inhibit the expression of the usual sort of responses and, in this way, allowing an opportunity for substitutive reconditioning to occur. This can be done only by means of coercive restraint and by restructuring the conflict situation, but it is only possible in those instances where the existing response is sufficiently flexible to be blocked by some more prepotent source of conflict. A response which is sufficiently rigid and intense--for example, an intense drive toward self-destruction--is not amenable to change under coercive conditions for the simple reason that coercion itself will ordinarily serve to aggravate and therefore to reinforce the intensity of the drive itself.

In most cases, some more pressing source of stress _is_ available and can be utilized to bring about a reorganization of the immediate hierarchy of values and therefore of the perceptual field. If the response to be altered is situational, stemming from purely objective factors--for example, as in the rat experiments conducted by Maier--three basic steps are required.

1) The subject must be restrained from performing the fixed-response. He must be subjected to sufficient countervailing frustration (punishment) to discourage any tendencies toward the response which is to he extinguished.

2) The original conflict-situation must be restructured in such a way as to call for a new type of response to the same stimulus situation.

3) The new response must be elicited and confirmed by means of either frustration- induced or motivation-induced learning. If the response to be eliminated is characterological (internalized and pervasive)--as, for example, in alcoholism--the method to be employed remains substantially the same as if it were situational but is vastly complicated by the difficulty of exercising practical control over the psychological stimuli which are capable of arousing the undesirable behavior as well as by the difficulties inherent in restructuring and reinforcing an alternative type of behavior.

Perhaps the basic criticism which has been leveled against this concept of frustration-induced learning is that it does not actually represent a different type of learning at all but is merely a variation of the usual goal-induced learning. In this sense, it has been pointed out that Maier's rats were not learning as a result of being punished but, rather, as a result of being partially reinforced (regardless of the card chosen) by being allowed to escape the punishing blast of air. From this point of view, the basic problem faced by the rat was how to augment reinforcement by passing from the relatively negative reward of avoiding further punishment to the more positive reward of actually gaining access to the food.

In a sense, of course, this is true. On the other hand, it overlooks several key points.

While the rat was reinforced on each trial by escaping the jet of air, he was not reinforced on each trial by being fed. Since the response-set of the rat encompassed a desire both to escape the air jet and to be fed, those trials where the rat jumped to the incorrect platform were experienced as negatively reinforcing as compared to those where his choice was correct and where he was allowed access to the food as well. In other words, relative to the total situation, these responses were experienced as ineffective and therefore nonreinforcing and not merely as additional partial reinforcements. The choice to jump consistently in one direction or the other was, in all events, a purely fortuitous choice elicited by such things as the sequence, proportion and interval of rewarded responses on each side of the platform. One alternative or the other was, purely on chance, destined to become dominant and subsequently to be confirmed through the effects of partial reinforcement.

In a sense, the situation with the rat and the stimulus-cards can be productively compared to the situation faced by many chronically deprived ghetto-children. Many ghetto-reared children are the products of negative social conditioning under chaotic circumstances. Like the rat, they have a constant air jet consisting of feelings of fear and hopelessness compounded by continuous frustration and a sense of inadequacy. As many see their situations, they have two basic alternatives: staying in school and facing constant humiliation or turning to the immediate gratifications offered by the highly dangerous world of drugs and antisocial gangs.

The rat is faced with a forced-choice situation in which he is confronted with a severely restricted number of predefined alternatives. He can jump to either the right or the left. He is forced to jump by two types of stress (motivation): (1) the specific stress associated with the air jet and (2) the more generalized stress growing out of his hunger. He is, moreover, confronted with a situation in which no objectively "good solution" is possible; there is no way of avoiding punishment regardless of what he does. As a result, the nature of the problem itself tends to be altered. After the rat has responded to this "impossible" situation for a period of time, the cumulative effects of being punished by the air jet and of the failure to obtain food, combined with the anxiety entailed by falling into the net-- an effect augmented by occasional reinforcements-- generates a heightened sense of anxiety which causes the rats anticipation of punishment to outweigh his anticipation of reward.

When this occurs, the rat develops the sort of compulsive anticipatory-response described by Maier. He cannot escape the situation. He can, however, escape <u>worrying about it</u> by responding to it <u>automatically</u>. He cannot escape the anguish entailed by his behavior. He can, however, escape the anguish of <u>choosing</u> his behavior. In a sense, of course, the rat has made an excellent "choice" by not choosing at all. Since he is faced with the sort of two-pronged decision in which one alternative is as likely to succeed as the other, he has inadvertently selected the most "rational" choice as well as the one which is psychologically expedient. By continuing to act, but by doing so ritualistically, the rat has managed to avoid the punishing jet of air, to obtain the highest possible chance proportion of successful jumps and to vent his tensions through activity. If he had failed to jump, none of these rewards would have been forthcoming. In effect, then, the rat has "learned" that it is better to do something and to fail <u>part</u> of the time than to do nothing and to fail <u>all</u> of the time.

Hierarchies: Psychological and Philosophical

There are essentially two ways of viewing human nature: (1) philosophically and (2) psychologically.

Philosophically, looking at man from the perspective of a total lifetime and within his natural and social context, it is clear that man's highest and most developed capacity resides in his capacity for symbolic reason as this is reflected in logical analysis, imagination and creativity (as well as the various combinations and permutations of these). Psychologically, it is clear that any individual's nature at any particular point in his development is radically contingent on the biological preconditions that provide the necessary basis for the realization of his rational nature (his self-actualizing needs). There is a natural "hierarchy of prepotency" that determines the evolution of selfhood toward incipient self-actualization at the rational/symbolic level. Biological needs precede and provide the necessary basis for the emotional needs, which, in turn, provide the necessary precondition for effective self-expression at the rational and symbolic level. Subjectivity (personality) is relative to the interplay of needs that are dictated psychologically by the very nature of the organism and the world in which this organism resides.

Reason is not in conflict with man's biological and emotional nature. At basis individual reason evolves psychologically out of a substructure of <u>nonrational</u> (but implicitly <u>rational</u>) behavior in the earliest weeks and months of life.

6. Autonomy I

The self-actualizing person is autonomous in the only meaningful sense of the term. He is not a solipsist who views autonomy as pure subjectivism. Rather, he accepts the given constraints of natural laws (including the empirical law of cause-and-effect, which is perhaps the most basic of the natural laws) as well as the indirect natural laws of logic itself (which are actually secondary natural laws in the sense that they are principles relating to intellectual discourse and not descriptions of necessary events in the natural world itself). At a psychological level, he accepts the fact that all behavior is motivated either conatively (by tacit need) or volitionally (by cognized signs or symbols of desired objects or events). He defers to the logical laws of excluded middle and non-contradiction, and accepts the facts that he cannot both want and not want the same thing at the same time (although he may vacillate very quickly and for extended periods of time between wanting and not wanting the same thing) and that he cannot want what he does not want (and vice versa).

In short, he recognizes that his freedom resides primarily in recognizing the necessity of subordinating himself to the objective requirements of the situation, to the constraints of reason, to using reason to adapt to reality, and to using comprehended reality as an instrument to make reality even more comprehensible and to make personal reason even more capable of comprehending it. Phrased somewhat differently, then, he uses his passion for objectivity as the central way in which he participates in the world, and in so doing, he not only perceives the world as it is but assimilates objectivity into his own subjective processes and, coincidentally, objectifies his own subjectivity.

In a sense, while retaining his unique differences, which are the unavoidable product of his own individual experiences in the world, his subjectivity (personality) becomes increasingly a "participational self," a part-function of reality in general. His commitment to objectivity-- to knowing and relating to the world-as-it-is--can be viewed as a sort of "objective love," a categorical concern with Being conceived in the broadest sort of terms in which his characteristic concern for others as others (altruism) is but one significant aspect.

Social Self

As a consequence of his objective subjectivity, the self-actualizing person recognizes that man, in his highest expression, is necessarily a part-function of others, that self-actualization is virtually always contingent upon social self-actualization.

Self-Actualization/Science

His pursuit of objective understanding inevitably leads him to understand that the closest epistemological counterpart of personal autonomy on an institutionalized, social basis is science. Science is the passionate pursuit of objective knowledge through a rigorous desubjectification of the knowing process. As in self-actualization, the passion for scientific truth is a heuristic passion which is, at best, both self-directing and self correcting.

Scientific Ethics

There is, as philosopher Jacob Bronowski points out in his book Science and Human Values, an ethic implicit within science, fully conceived. The scientist as a scientist has a prepotent passion for scientific knowledge, an overriding commitment to a particular type of truth, to a truth determined and defined through the scientific process. Fully understood, this kind of knowledge exists independent of and takes precedence over the various other beliefs and opinions of scientists who are committed to this overriding passion. Indeed, it addresses itself indirectly to one of the central--if not <u>the</u> central--quandary within traditional philosophy: How is it possible to separate <u>fact</u> from <u>value</u>, <u>isness</u> from <u>oughtness</u>? It can be (and is) done, states Bronowski, by the simple expedient of defining <u>truth</u> as the overriding <u>value</u> to be sought--provided that one has defined truth primarily as a particular process of inquiry that demands no less than the total subordination of all subjectivity to a particular definition of objectivity. In short, the scientific ethic <u>is</u> scientific objectivity.

But such an ethic is necessarily evolving, incomplete, and relative--as, science itself is evolving, incomplete and relative. How does one determine a programmatic social ethic replete with imperatives that govern interpersonal behavior on such a broad basis? Neither Bronowski nor Maslow himself (in his <u>Psychology of Science</u>) address themselves directly to this question, but the answer is clearly implied. If such a social ethic is not directly stated, the process of deriving such an ethic is relatively obvious. Science can analyze the nature of man as man and the nature of men in society. Science can analyze the nature of the world and of reality-in-general.

The optimum relationship between what man requires and what society is capable of providing can be determined by interpreting existing scientific knowledge. In a similar sense, the optimum relationship between human needs (both individual and social) and the possibilities for satisfying such needs that are available in the natural world can be determined in general outline. In short, social ethics can be determined scientifically by determining the optimum relationship between the nature of man, the nature of society (as properly conceived) and the nature of the natural world as all of these are scientifically understood at any particular time.

In making these determinations, five considerations must be taken into account:

1) The dominant scientific paradigm is implicitly founded upon certain philosophical assumptions. Science is empirical, behavioristic, and materialistic.

2) Science is open and evolving. It does not sanction terminal certitude in the area of social ethics. The scientific ethic always takes precedence over any programmatic social ethic derived from science itself.

3) However objective the subjectivity of a scientist may be, science is still at basis subjective. Science solves problems, and problems--however experimentally they may be resolved--are not <u>perceived</u> "scientifically." In short, scientists study what they look at, and what they look at is determined by their interests, which are, in turn, determined by characterological and situational factors that are only indirectly involved with "science" as such. Problem-solving is contingent on problem-perceiving, which is always skewed to some extent by character (even in the self-actualizing). Only the perceptions of a multiplicity of different scientists over a very long period of time is likely to balance out.

4) As Maslow clearly recognizes in his book <u>The Psychology of Science</u> there are three basic expressions of science: (1) normative science, (2) non-normative science and (3) anti-normative science. <u>Normative science</u> (as in humanistic psychology) is science used intentionally and explicitly to comprehend the nature of man and the social/moral implications of this nature. <u>Non-normative science</u> (as in particle physics) is science used to explore the natural world but with no direct, intentional, and explicit concern with determining the nature of man and the social/moral implications of this nature in any immediate sense. <u>Anti-normative science</u> is used as a "flight to reality," as a means of gathering more or less meaningless data (data which bears no significant relationship to significant human problems) as a way of avoiding any confrontation with significant human problems or with knowledge which impacts significantly on such problems.

5) Since large aspects of reality cannot be controlled and therefore resist attempts at scientific analysis, science can at best be approximated in many situations--as in clinical psychology or in participant-observer research in the area of anthropology. At the present time, the scientific study of man and society is probably

necessarily a combination of "hard" (experimental) science and "soft" (clinical or non-experimental) science. (Actually, Maslow was a representative of neither of these positions. He was, if anything, a sort of "soft" behaviorist in the sense that he was willing to go beyond the study of behavior as such and make theoretical inferences that go far beyond the relatively cautious ideas offered by such "hard" behaviorists as John Watson and B. F. Skinner.)

As a causal principle, self-actualization is more basic than science, because science is explicable as a particular expression of self-actualization but not vice versa.

Science/Pragmatism

Science, as a form of closely controlled experimentalism, is implicitly pragmatic. The experiment works if its consequences are effective, if it solves the problem at hand. The ultimate verification, however, resides in the emotional/hedonic effects of behavior vis-à-vis defined problems that relate to defined goals.

Phrased somewhat differently, science, like self-actualization itself, ultimately rests on the pleasure principle. Science can be used as one means of attaining self-actualization, but self-actualization, as a far broader and more encompassing category of behavior, cannot be viewed as one aspect of science. In a sense, science is always (psychologically) a <u>means</u>. Self-actualization, on the other hand, is, in a broad sense, an <u>end</u>.

Social Self-Actualization/Science

The ideal society would, in this sense, probably be a society of self-actualizing scientists studying individual and social human behavior as it relates to self-actualization and related topics. Barring this, it would probably be a society organized along the principles determined by a subculture directed to this pursuit.

Growth Motivation/Autonomy

If the organism is allowed to follow its own psychological logic, allowing the various categories of needs to evolve and develop in a natural developmental sequence, the nature and content of the internal reality (subjectivity) that coalesces out of a natural sequence of need-gratifications will be substantially different than what occurs under conditions of need-deprivation or need-frustration. The satisfaction of prepotent physical and psychological needs allows the individual to perceive the world through a subjectivity that is essentially non-refracting, that is, capable of responding more or less spontaneously to the sort of patternality (meaning) that inheres within the situation rather than projecting its own prepotent psychological needs (with all of their relatively subjective content) upon the situation. He becomes, in a sense, free to act <u>within</u> the situation rather than <u>upon</u> it. Freed from pressing emotional requirements, his "objective subjectivity" is capable of participating in the world as-it-is rather than forcing it to address itself as an obtrusive and alien "otherness."

Perceptual Accuracy

The key to self-actualization is perceptual accuracy. The only general requirement for the self-actualizing person is to be fully alive fully realized in the one realm of his being, his rational-symbolic nature that remains relatively undeveloped. From this point of view, other things being equal, his development will be determined by an "open" system of reason and related rational-symbolic processes that will both reinforce his previously attained state of biological and emotional gratification and, at the same time, augment and perfect both his own rational nature and (indirectly) the rationality of the world in which he resides.

7. Knowledge

Knowledge as Direct Participation

The basic error implicit in most theories of self-actualization stems from an artificially narrow concept of <u>self</u>--and, more particularly, from an erroneous concept of <u>mind.</u>

Mind (experience) is not an entity. Rather, it is an active relation of entities, a "being-in-the-world," in which "the person and his world are a unitary, structural whole" (May 1967:59). As psychologist Erich Fromm indicates:

"Knowledge is not obtained in the position of the split between subject and object, but in the position of relatedness. As Goethe put it: 'Man knows himself only inasmuch as he knows the world. He knows the world only within himself, and he is aware of himself only within the world.' Each new object, truly recognized, opens up a new organ within ourselves" (Fromm 1962:73).

Human experience is based upon two underlying components: (1) the "internal reality" of the <u>self</u> which provides the psychological, or subjective, pole of the experiential continuum, and (2) the "external reality" of the natural world which provides the ontological, or objective, whole.

Since the self is but one aspect of the natural world and can be comprehended only in its terms, as a byproduct of involvement, self and nature can actually be regarded as comprising conceptually divisible aspects of what is actually an indivisible totality of interrelated forces.

Human experience is implicitly teleological, for, as philosopher Eliseo Vivas states, "the notion of an 'organism' entails functions of its component organs, controlled by the type or form" (Vivas 1963:59) and "innate potentiality and latent powers are clearly telic in nature" (Vivas 1963:64). "A 'need' or a 'drive' is not a blind lack which any object will satisfy but a structured lack addressed toward a determinate class of objects" (Vivas 1963:60).

In the final analysis, human experience (and therefore human knowledge) is directed and channelized by two underlying factors: (1) that which is (ontologically) knowable and (2) that which is (psychologically) capable of being known. Since knowledge is always a concomitant of goal-oriented instrumental behavior, knowledge is always implicitly committed to the realization of certain purposes, and the "experiential elements of a commitment cannot be defined in non-committal terms" (Polanyi 1958: 379). In other words, all knowledge is, as Polanyi puts it, unavoidably "personal knowledge" (Polanyi 1958:passim).

Human experience is then determined by structure-function and grows out of a total and unified field of forces, both internal and external. As Spinoza observed: "It is impossible for a man not to be a part of nature and not to follow its general order" (Smith and Debbins 1948:35).

The mind does not exist apart from the world but, quite the contrary, is basically isomorphic with it. Experience grows out of behavior. Behavior is, in turn, conditioned by the objective requirements of self and environment, and such requirements are precisely the conditions necessary for any sort of personal experience to occur at all. At basis, then, and as psychologist Joseph Royce states "...there is a functional representation in the brain which corresponds to a specific structural arrangement at the phenomenological or behavior level" (Royce 1964:95).

The nature of experience is contingent on the nature of objective reality. The human organism is inherently conative. Conation, expressed in terms of inherent potentialities for behavior, better expressed in the light of existing circumstances, gives rise to personal experience and yields personal knowledge.

In a sense, then, potentialities affect knowledge in two ways. First, they determine the course of knowledge by determining access to behavior. Second, by becoming known indirectly through behavior, they become a form of self-knowledge which, accordingly, serves to redirect subsequent behavior and subsequent experience/learning as well.

In the final analysis, then, behavior is determined morphogenetically by the objective realities of predetermined structure-function. Life is intrinsically dynamic, oriented to the satisfaction of certain inherent biological needs. As Harold Rugg states, there is a general character which pervades all organic form.

Since individuals' inherent needs can be realized only through the expression of innate potentialities, the realization of innate potentialities is also an implied need (and therefore an implied value as well). Psychological research confirms, for example, that even acute sensory - and perceptual - deprivation is almost invariably psychopathogenic in its effects.

At basis, function is caused by structure, and the nature of the self acts not only as a possibility for action but also as an imperative toward certain acts. As the mind is ultimately total and holistic, so knowledge is ultimately configurational and interdependent. In the evolution of human thought, we ordinarily grasp things as wholes before we grasp their constituent elements. Indeed, in the evolution of personal knowledge, behavior as such necessarily precedes a conscious knowledge of such behavior.

Our first and formative consciousness is always a consciousness of total patterns of response that were formed pre-cognitively as a reaction to objective structural imperatives growing out of given situations that were encountered during the earliest weeks and months of life. Thus, we learn to sing before we learn to read music. Indeed, we are capable of learning to read music only because we know what music "means"--that is, only because the total pattern ("singing") already exists and therefore makes the component elements (the notes, the time, and so on) which comprise its analytical constituents "meaningful" as focal objects for subsequent study. In learning to read music, as in any cognitive activity, the simpler elements can be comprehended only in terms of the cognitively more complex behavioral patterns which psychologically occur first. "A comprehensive entity," states Polanyi, "is something else than its particulars known focally, in themselves" (Polanyi 1960:65). "We can know a successful system only by understanding it as a whole, while being subsidiarily aware of its particulars; and we cannot meaningfully study these particulars except with a bearing on the whole" (Polanyi 1958:381).

"It is not surprising ... that we may often apprehend wholes without ever having focally attended to their particulars. In such cases we are actually ignorant, or perhaps more precisely speaking, focally ignorant of these particulars; we know them only subsidiarily in terms of what they jointly mean, but cannot tell what they are in themselves. Practical skills and practical experience contain much more information than people possessing this expert knowledge can ever tell" (Polanyi 1960:32-33).

Mature "wisdom" consists precisely of the capacity to transcend what Polanyi terms the focal awareness of partial knowledge and to return, through a global cognitive relationing of hitherto discrete information, to a renewed appreciation of more general meanings. In such instances, and as Polanyi states:

"... the focus of our attention is shifted from the hitherto uncomprehended particulars to the understanding of their joint meaning. This shift of attention does not make us lose sight of the particulars since one can see a whole only by seeing its parts, but it changes altogether the manner in which we are aware of the particulars. We become aware of them now in terms of the whole on which we have fixed our attention" (Polanyi 1960:29-30).

In a similar sense, a tacit knowledge of a comprehensive entity (such as a knowledge of the human organism itself) and a knowledge of its particulars (such as a knowledge of the inner ear or of the hand) are fundamentally incompatible, because they represent two distinct levels of reality. An attempt to define a Gestalt in terms of its own constituents is basically misconceived, because the elements of a Gestalt are necessarily grasped by means of <u>subsidiary awareness</u> and any attempt to impose <u>focal awareness</u> upon them destroys the basic relationship which they <u>are</u>. As Polanyi indicates, then, "<u>Dismemberment</u> of a comprehensive entity <u>produces</u> <u>incomprehension</u> of it and in this sense the entity is logically unspecifiable in terms of its particulars" (Polanyi 1960:45).

If "mind" cannot be equated with the human organism, it stands to reason that rationality is not limited to man but extends to the non-human environment as well. Indeed, and as Allstadl so eloquently argued, an intelligent organism implies an intelligible universe.

As biologist E. S. Russell states, "Instead of attempting to explain the 'teleological' nature of organic activities in terms of concepts derived from man's knowledge of his own purposive activity, as do the mechanist and the vitalist, we should take precisely the opposite view, and regard human purposive activities (including machine-making) and modes or thought as being a specialized development of the fundamental 'purposiveness' or as I prefer to call it, the directiveness and creativeness, of life" (Russell, cited in Rugg 1963:121).

In a sense, then, mind is cosmic and not purely human. The human brain is merely the instrumentality through which objective mind (that is, the rationality of nature as such) manifests itself <u>to</u> <u>itself</u> as a means of modifying its own function. Progress is, in this respect, not illusory, as is frequently maintained, but real. As theologian Paul Tillich states: "Mans productivity moves from potentiality to actuality in such a way that everything actualized has potentialities for further actualization. This is the basic structure of progress" (Tillich 105).

Knowledge as creative

Reality is organismic and interdependent, and, within this reality, man functions as a specialized agent of awareness--a sort of cosmic cerebral cortex--which has the capacity to objectify the implicit and, in so doing, to regulate, within limits, the nature and conditions of reality itself. "The infants understanding of its surroundings is self-centered. It goes on plunging irreversibly from one form of comprehension to another. Then, gradually, it develops a solid interpretative framework, each successive stage of which offers a possibility for increasingly elaborate logical operations. Irreversible comprehension is replaced by the steady deployment of discursive thought. The appetitive, motoric, perceptive child is transformed into an intelligent person, reasoning with universal intent. We have here a process of maturation closely analogous to the corresponding step of anthropogenetic emergence, leading from the self-centered individuality of the animal to the responsible personhood of thoughtful man; in fact, to the emergence of the noosphere. (Polanyi 1958:395).

The more a person learns, the more he is capable of transmitting (through the extragenetic heredity afforded by symbolic learning) thereby expediting and advancing still more knowledge. In the eloquent words of Bernard Shaw's <u>Don Juan,</u>

"... I, my friend, am as much a part of Nature as my own finger is a part of me. If my finger is the organ by which I grasp the sword and the mandolin, my brain is the organ by which Nature strives to understand itself. My dog's brain serves only my dog's purposes; but my own brain labors at a knowledge which does nothing for me personally but makes my body better to me in my decay and death a calamity. Were 1 not possessed with a purpose beyond my own I had better be a ploughman than a philosopher; for the ploughman lives as long as the philosopher, eats more, sleeps better, and rejoices in the wife of his bosom with less misgiving. This is because the philosopher is in the grip of the Life Force. This Life Force says to him I have done a thousand wonderful things unconsciously by merely willing to live and following the line of least resistance: now I want to know myself and my destination, and choose my paths; so I have made a special brain--a philosopher's brain--to grasp knowledge for me as the husbandman's hand grasps the plow for me. 'And this,' says the Life Force to the philosopher, 'must thou strive to do for me until thou diest, when I will make another brain and another philosopher to carry on the work'"(Shaw 141).

If man is properly characterized as intrinsically <u>active</u>, so <u>all</u> of reality is intrinsically active. The world itself is, at basis, both dynamic and purposive. If it were not purposive, it would not be comprehensible, for, as Polanyi indicates, a true understanding of anything is necessarily predicated upon some assumptions about its underlying purpose (the overall design of its ongoing behavior) and, without such information, all other information remains meaningless (Polanyi 1960:52). "Take a watch to pieces and examine, however carefully, its separate parts in turn, and you will never come across the principles by which a watch keeps time. This may sound trivial; but is actually of decisive significance" (Polanyi 1960:47).

The study of an organ must begin with an attempt to guess what it is for and how it works. Only then can we proceed further by combined physiological and physico-chemical enquiries. Both being conducted with a bearing on the purposive physiological framework which they help to elucidate. Any attempt to conduct physico-chemical investigations of a living being irrespective of physiological assumptions will lead as a rule to meaningless results; and any attempt to replace physiology altogether by a physico-chemical chart of the living organism would completely dissolve any understanding of the organism. (Polanyi 1958:360)

We have a solid tangible inanimate object before us--let us say a grandfather clock. But we do not know what it is. Then let a team of physicists and chemists inspect the object. Let them be equipped with all the physics and chemistry ever to be known, but let their technological outlook be that of the stone age. Or, if we cannot disregard the practical incompatibility of these two assumptions, let us agree that in their investigations they shall not refer to any operational principles. They will describe the clock precisely in every particular, and in addition, will predict all its possible future configurations. Yet they will never be able to tell us that it is a clock. <u>The complete knowledge of a machine as an object tells us nothing about it as a machine.</u>

"... If any object--such as, for example, a machine--is essentially characterized by a comprehensive feature, then our understanding of this feature will grant us a true knowledge of what the object is. It will reveal a machine as a machine. But the observation of the same object in terms of physics and chemistry will spell complete ignorance of what it is. Indeed, the more detailed knowledge we acquire of a thing, the more our attention is distracted from seeing what it is" (Polanyi 1958:330-333).

"A complete physical and chemical topography of a frog would tell us nothing about it as a frog, unless we knew it previously <u>as a frog</u>" (Polanyi 1958:342).

"...the meaning of an animal's actions can be understood only by reading the particulars of its actions (or by reading its mind in terms of these actions) and not by observing the actions themselves as we may observe inanimate processes" (Polanyi 1958:364).

"... a knowledge of physics and chemistry would in itself not enable us to recognize a machine. Suppose you are faced with a problematic object and try to explore its nature by a meticulous physical or chemical analysis of its parts.... The questions: 'Does the thing serve any purpose, then if so, what purpose, and how does it achieve it?' can be answered only by testing the object practically as a possible instance of known, or conceivable, machines. The physico-chemical topography of the object may in some cases serve as a clue to its technical interpretation, but by itself it would leave us completely in the dark in this respect" (Polanyi 1958:330).

In a profound sense, then, and as Polanyi suggests, "...all meaning lies in the comprehension of a set of particulars in terms of a coherent entity" (Polanyi 1960:49). Reality can be characterized as "rational," as "making sense precisely because it is characteristically directed toward certain ends rather than others. At basis, these ends are to be discovered in rationality itself, for the basic principles of logic are nothing more than the controlling relationships which govern the behavior of reality as such. An irrational world would not be purposive precisely because it would not be objectively "committed" to any predictable course of action. Reality is teleological because the present is as inevitably determined (or caused) by the future as it is by the past. In a sense, then, the future is inherent in the present and provides the encompassing plan for all change.

At basis, then, reality is purposive. It grows out of the unavoidable requirements of objective processes in continuous interrelationship. To the extent that these processes change or their relationships alter, "reality" changes as well. Truth, which cognitively reflects reality, is also purposive. Since cognition is invariably practical and goal-oriented, the great general "truths"--the laws of physical science, the theorems of geometry, and such--are nothing more than principles which serve to advance effective (functional) behavior in the long run.

In a sense, of course, since all structure implies function and since all function implies intent (or purpose), all general truths, being statements about the nature, or structure, of Being, are also statements of intent and therefore statements of value as well as of fact. To say, for example, that "Man is rational" is to say, in essence, (1) that man has the capacity for rational action; (2) that man functions rationally as evidence of such capacity; (3) that rational behavior is used as a device for realizing human ends; (4) that rationality is therefore an instrumental value; and (5) that rational behavior is therefore good. Ultimately, then, there is nothing mystical about intuitive "felt-thought." It is subject to pragmatic verification like all other thought. Since learning is mediated by reward (pleasure or pain), the only direct verification of truth is by means of experienced value, or pleasure.

It is the nature of the human organism to seek pleasure and therefore to seek knowledge with respect to those conditions which are deemed to be requirements for the realization of optimized pleasure which come to be viewed as <u>objective values</u>.

Morality--viewed as the intentional pursuit of objective value--can only be limited, then, by ignorance. Perfect knowledge (as Socrates maintained) would invariably yield perfect morality as well.

On the other hand, the objectively good is apprehensible only on the basis of subjective, or personal, experience, and a knowledge of objective good can be obscured by a vast range of intervening circumstances. <u>Practical morality</u> is seldom viewed as synonymous with <u>objective morality</u>, because, since personal knowledge is seldom very objective, the demands of objective morality are not often considered to be consistent with the requirements of practical behavior. Accordingly, practical behavior is generally a prudential compromise on the basis of anticipated consequences between that which is deemed objectively (or ultimately) good and that which is deemed practically (or proximately) good.

With respect to self-actualization perhaps the outstanding virtue accruing to self- gratification is that it provides a release from the usual sorts of purely circumstantial, or "stimulus-bound" motivation so characteristic of the need-deprived. In so doing, it invests the individual with perhaps the fundamental condition required to pursue objective (or non-circumstantial) value more or less regardless of particular circumstances.

Phrased somewhat differently, the self-actualizing person, being relieved of the necessity of perceiving reality in a narrowly instrumental (or deficiency-motivated) fashion, finds himself in the enviable situation of being able to seek objective (situationally-congruous) values without going through the usual process of adapting these to the demands of more compelling deficiency requirements.

True self-actualizing behavior is primarily expressive and only secondarily goal oriented. For such people, and to use the Kantian terminology, the categorical imperative is capable of functioning as a hypothetical imperative as well. They can trust their impulses and intuitions to be "moral" for the simple reason that they have substantially nothing to gain from what might otherwise appear to be tempting, immoral behavior. Like the "superior man" described in the Analects of Confucius, such a person is capable of "[going] through life without any preconceived course of action or any taboo. He merely decides for the moment what is the right thing to do" (Watts 1958:151).

"It was for this reason," states Watts, "that Confucius made Zen or 'human-heartedness' a far higher virtue than i or 'righteousness,' and declined to give the former any clear definition. For man cannot define or legalize his own nature. He may attempt to do so only at the cost of identifying himself with an abstract and incomplete image of himself--that is, with a mechanical principle which is qualitatively inferior to a man. Thus Confucius felt that in the long run human passions and feelings were more trustworthy than human principles of right and wrong, that the natural man was more of a man than the conceptual man, the constructed person.

Principles were excellent, and indeed necessary, so long as they were tempered with human-heartedness and the sense of proportion or humour that goes with it. War, for example, is less destructive when fought for greed than for the justifications of ideological principles, since greed will not destroy what it wishes to possess, whereas, the vindication of principle is an abstract goal which is perfectly ruthless in regard to the humane values of life, limb, and property" (Watts 1958:150).

If intuition is pragmatic, however, it is verified, not analytically, but rather existentially to a continuous sort of total organismic feedback in which "we rely on tacit performances of our own, the rightness of which we implicitly confirm" (Polanyi 1958:100).

The sign of successful intuition is not a symbolic proof, but a <u>completed act</u>, one which has resulted in a synthesis of ideo-motor-affective unity. True knowledge is more likely to be learned and, hence, disseminated than the false for the simple reason that it is more effective and therefore more frequently reinforced. As Rugg states:

"The feedback element, built into the stored data of organized human experience (memory) becomes an enormously intricate fusion of cortical-cell-assembly, of tensile dynamics in the musculature, of release of endocrine secretions in the circulating bloodstream, and of overt as well as incipient movements in the eyes, head, arms, hands, torso. The nub of the complex process is the organism's attempt to perceive (partly visual, partly muscular response in the torso, I think) the relations of parts that will produce the felt (imagined) organization.

"In problem-solving this adjusting process does indeed seem to act in the manner of feedback, reflected in cut-and-try oscillations before the correct adjustment is hit upon. Some phases of it can be seen also in the first stages of the creative process of the painter, writer, dancer, or musician: the improvising of a first statement...its comparison (a total body-response) with the imagined conception...the putting down of the new bit of color or shifting of line, mass, or texture...it's bodily appraisal, again with a new imagined conception as the norm.... oscillations of adjustments (sets or attitudes of anticipation), all tending to come to a more stable rest along a line of direction" (Rugg 1963:256)

This means that all forms of intellectual verification--scientific, pragmatic, positivistic, and so on--are necessarily subordinate to prior assumptions derived on the basis of pre-rational behavior. "The greatest error, from the Renaissance to our own day," states Ortega, "lay in believing--with Descartes--that we live out of our consciousness, that slight portion of our being that we see clearly and upon which our will operates. To say that man is rational and free is, I think, a statement very close to being false. We actually do possess reason and freedom; but both powers form only a tenuous film which envelopes our being, the interior of which is neither rational nor free. The ideas, of which reason is composed, come to us ready-made from a vast, obscure source located beneath our consciousness" (Ortega 1960:84-5).

Most of what we know remains in the form of what Polanyi terms <u>tacit knowledge</u> and even <u>explicit knowledge</u>, and is largely contingent upon prior tacit assumptions. As Polanyi states "...tacit knowing is in fact the dominant principle of all knowledge, and ... its rejection would, therefore, automatically involve the rejection of any knowledge whatever" (Polanyi 1960:13).

Tacit knowledge is inarticulate, because it is implicit within all behavior. It is unspecifiable in terms of its own particulars, and it is not usually accorded the exalted status of true "knowledge" at all.

8. Autonomy II

In self-actualization, cognition, conation, and affect are far more synergistic than antagonistic, and this fact is reflected in a variety of ways, ranging all the way from creativity (which is tied in with perceptual efficiency and with the capacity to function without rubricized thought, among other things) to a significant capacity for "accepting" (i.e.. perceiving) the world as it really is.

Self-actualization theory is founded upon the basic precepts of behavioral determinism, and the fundamental assumption of all determinism is that for every event there is a set of conditions which, if repeated, would result in a repetition of the same event. The sort of personal autonomy which emerges out of self-actualization is in no sense opposed to this principle. As philosopher Abraham Kaplan states, "That man is free does not mean that he stands outside the causal network, but that the causes working on him work <u>through</u> him, that is, through his knowledge of causes and effects" (Kaplan 1963:250).

The principle of causality itself is implicitly deterministic. There is, from a purely causal point of view--and Andre Gide notwithstanding--no such thing as purely <u>gratuitous</u> <u>action.</u>

This does not, however, preclude the possibility of a certain type and degree of human <u>self</u>-determination. A person is capable of intentionally (purposefully) directing his own behavior within limits, of acting voluntaristically with respect to his own recognized goals or "motives."

<u>Determinism</u> is not, in other words, the same thing as <u>fatalism</u>, and, as philosopher John Hospers indicates, "Determinism does not say that every event is caused by conditions outside our control but only that every event is caused; and causation is quite compatible with some causes being <u>ourselves</u>, our decisions, our acts of willing, our desires to do this or that" (Hospers 1961:503).

In this sense, mechanistic causation is a necessary, but scarcely sufficient, explanation of human behavior. As Gilbert Ryle comments in his book <u>The Concept of Mind</u>:

"The favourite model to which the fancied mechanistic world is assimilated is that of billiard balls imparting their motion to one another by impact. Yet a game of billiards provides one of the simplest examples of the course of events for the description of which mechanical terms are necessary without being sufficient. Certainly from accurate knowledge of the weight, shape, elasticity and movements of the balls, the constitution of the table and the conditions of the atmosphere it is in principle possible, in accordance with known laws, to deduce from a momentary state of the balls what will be their later state. But it does not follow from this that the course of the game is predictable in accordance with those laws alone.

"...the billiards player asks for no special indulgences from the laws of physics any more than he does from the rules of billiards. Why should he? They do not force his hand. The fears expressed by some moral philosophers that the advance of the natural sciences diminishes the field within which the moral virtues can be exercised rests on the assumption that there is some contradiction in saying that one and the same occurrence is governed both by mechanical laws and by moral principles, an assumption as baseless as the assumption that a golfer cannot at once conform to the laws of ballistics <u>and</u> obey the rules of golf <u>and</u> play with arrogance and skill. Not only is there plenty of room for purpose where everything is governed by mechanical laws, but there would be no place for purpose if things were not so governed. Predictability is a necessary condition of planning" (Ryle 1949:80-81).

The hearsay knowledge that everything in Nature is subject to mechanical laws often tempts people to say that Nature is either one big machine, or else a conglomeration of machines. But in fact there are very few machines in Nature. The only machines we find are the machines that human beings make, such as clocks, windmills and turbines. There are a very few natural systems which somewhat resemble such machines, namely, such things as solar systems. They do not go on by themselves and repeat indefinitely the same series of movements. They do go, as few unmanufactured things do, "like clock-work". True, to make machines we have to know and apply Mechanics. But inventing machines is not copying things found in inanimate Nature.

Paradoxical though it may seem, we have to look rather to living organisms for examples in Nature of self-maintaining, routine-observing systems. The movements of the heavenly bodies provided one kind of "clock." It was the human pulse that provided the next. Nor is it merely primitive animism which makes native children think of engines as iron horses. There is very little else in Nature to which they are so closely analogous. Avalanches and games of billiards are subject to mechanical laws; but they are not at all like the workings of machines. (Ryle 1949:82)

A person who is intuitively attuned to life-as-process feels a sense of unity with his environment and does not experience himself as the objectified product of alienated forces catalogued in terms of "causes" and "effects." As the philosopher and theologian Alan Watts indicates:

"If we are to abandon Newtonian mechanics in the physical sphere we must also do so in the psychological and moral. In the same measure that the atoms are not billiard balls struck into motion by others, our actions are not entities forced into operation by distinct motives and drives. Actions appear to be forced by other things to the degree that the agent identifies himself with a single part of the situation in which the actions occur, such as the will as distinct from the passions, or the mind as distinct from the body. But if he identifies himself with his passions or with his body, he will not seem to be moved by them. If he can't go further and see that he is not simply his body but the whole of his body-environment relationship, he will not even feel forced to act by his environment. The effect appears to be controlled passively by its cause only insofar as it is considered to be distinct from the cause. But if cause and effect are just terms of a single act, there is neither controller nor controlled. Thus the feeling that action has to spring from necessity comes from thinking that the self is the center of consciousness as distinct from the periphery" (Watts 1957:111).

At still another point in his writings, Watts goes on to state that cause-and-effect is largely an academic answer to an academic question. Thus a child who is insecure for lack of love is not only insecure as an <u>effect</u>, but he is also hungry for love as <u>cause</u>, The two are inseparable aspects of the organic unity of a particular child in a particular environment. As Watts indicates:

"To say that the organism <u>needs</u> food is only to say that it <u>is</u> food. To say that it eats <u>because</u> it is hungry is only to say that it eats when it is ready to eat. To say that it dies because it cannot find food is only another way of saying that its death is the same thing as it ceasing to be consistent with its environment. The so-called causal explanation of an event is only the description of the same event in other words. To quote Wittgenstein... 'At the basis of the whole modern view of the world lies the illusion that the so-called laws of nature are the explanations of natural phenomena'" (Watts 1961: 27).

In a basic sense, then, man is "free to choose," but only within a predetermined framework established by his prior experience and limited by the knowledge created by this experience. He is free to pursue his own ends independent of immediate circumstantial determination, but he is not free to "choose himself," that is, to be the ultimate cause, or motive, behind his own final criteria for choice, behind his own governing self-system, which constitutes the controlling centrality in all of his behavior.

It can be argued, of course, that the "growth motives" exemplified in Maslow's hierarchy of prepotency are not "new" kinds of motives at all but merely extensions (or special kinds) of deficiency-motives because (1) they are motivated by need (for pleasure) and because (2) they are causally related in a developmental sense to earlier deficiency motives (necessarily evolving over a long period of time out of the sequential gratification of lower needs during the earliest weeks, months, and years of life).

In a sense, however, the argument over whether growth-motives are or are not "new" kinds of motives is simply a quibble over what is meant by the term "new." If something must be unrelated to (and therefore uncaused by) previous conditions to be "new," nothing can be new without violating the law of cause-and-effect. This is like saying that, if one tears down an old brick wall and uses the bricks to build a house, one does not have a house at all but merely a variation of the original wall. The point is that we call it a house not because it bears no relationship to a wall--it does, after all, share not only the bricks but also such common elements as color and texture, and both participate in such general conditions as the laws of structural dynamics--but rather because it constitutes a significantly different expression of the elements which are common to both.

Since all behavior is initially deficiency-motivated, it stands to reason that all subsequent behavior can ultimately be traced back to deficiency-motivated antecedents. On the other hand, this does not necessarily eventuate in the reductionist conclusion that something is nothing more than its lowest common denominator in the causal sequence of behavior. It is the way that behavior functions in the present not its historical or genetic determinants which is primarily significant in determining how and to what extent such behavior is causal. The fact that the body was initially a fertilized egg does not mean that it <u>remains</u> a fertilized egg or that it continues to <u>function</u> as a fertilized egg. In a similar sense, the fact that man's power of imagination is explicable on the basis of biological (electrochemical) processes does not mean that this is a <u>sufficient</u> description of what reasoning is or how it operates in any contemporary sense.

On the other hand, this is not to say that the motives which activate an individual's behavior are <u>de novo</u>. They are necessarily the outgrowth of certain types of prevoluntaristic experience (in the first instance) and must invariably reflect the nature of this predetermination in significant respects.

In short, while man is "free" to impose his motives on otherwise determining experience, and, in so doing, to project a certain sort of voluntaristic control over the present course of events, he is decidedly <u>not</u> free (as a necessarily predetermined personality) to be the originating agency behind the personality which, once determined, through the course of precognitive motor-emotional conditioning commit him to a certain course of action rather than another. These motives, however modified by subsequent experience they may be, remain essentially the product of behavioral conditioning in the earliest era of life, and all of a person's subsequent efforts do not allow him to transcend the sort of precognitive "imprinting" that occurred during the earliest and essentially prevolitional stages of his being.

At basis, then, however "reasonable" it may be, self-actualizing behavior is never <u>originally</u> the product of conscious and systematic reasoning. The perceptual accuracy, or objectivity, of the self-actualizer, once it has emerged, initiates and augments further self- actualizing behavior. In the final analysis, however, perceptual accuracy is merely one of the more significant effects of self-actualizing behavior and not its original cause. The same basic relationship holds true with such self-actualizing characteristics as spontaneity, rationality and autonomy. These too are best described as qualities associated with self-actualizing behavior and not (at least originally) as character traits which bring such behavior into being.

Phrased somewhat differently, then, in the case of self-actualization, it is the gratification of basic needs in the course of personal development which creates the conditions required for reasonable people and not the other way around. Self-actualization is never originally either the product of rational analysis or the outgrowth of a conscious commitment to truth in the abstract. Rather, in most instances, it evolves out of the <u>preverbal</u> processes of continuous and systematic gratification of prepotent developmental needs which occurred during the earliest years of life and which created the kind of sanity which made perceptual accuracy possible in the first instance.

Self- actualization leads to true values in a derivative sense, but, in a more significant sense, it is the emergence of true values that ultimately creates self-actualization. The sequence of events might be roughly outlined as follows:

True values (that is, values which are consonant with the innate demands of the organism)
 emerge out of the successful pursuit of
true goals (objects and events which are consonant with the innate demands of the organism during the developmental era
 which
contribute to effective behavior (which is experienced subjectively as pleasure)
 and which gives rise to
true knowledge
 including
more true goals
 which are also generalized to confirm and to expand the awareness of
true values

and so on , and so on.

Since all behavior is ultimately rooted in hedonic (pleasure-pain) activity, the same basic model might be represented as follows:

Effective (gratified) behavior
    gives rise to
pleasurable experience
    which is consolidated, over time, as
rational (effective) behavior
    which is interiorized as intrinsically
rational knowledge
    which
reinforces the desire for the same and similar types of behavior in the future
    which are also
confirmed and strengthened through their overwhelmingly pleasurable consequences
    and which are therefore preserved and perfected, serving to consolidate reason and future applications of rational behavior.

As Maslow sees it, any accurate theory of human motivation is necessarily a field theory. It is necessary to consider needs as they exist in relationship to external circumstances. Ultimately, it is not simply the nature of needs or potentialities but also the nature of the available conditions which indicates either the possibility or the probability of any particular sort of activity. Phrased somewhat differently, what any individual learns in the process of self-development is not "values" in the abstract but, rather, the utility and effectiveness of certain types of goal-directed activity that only gradually comes to be construed as implying the existence and necessity of certain types of values on a more abstract level. (Maslow 1970:120)

In the final analysis, self-actualization is not merely a realization of potential but, rather, a realization of certain specific potentialities (such as the capacity for love or creativity) and the corollary denial of others (such as the capacity for unreasoned hate or for blind social conformity).

Accordingly, such potentialities are meaningful only in terms of some recognized worldview. At basis, then, self-actualization is a psychology which presupposes a certain type of ontology. The good is to be found in one's nature, but human nature is inextricably related to, and can be defined only in terms of, those impersonal conditions which are required for the maintenance of personal existence (including, by implication, sustained self-other relationships). In a broader sense, then, self-actualization necessarily entails the realization of others, and, even, the perfection of the world in general through a process of emergent evolution. In this sense, self-actualization requires not so much a description of the self per se as a concept of the total human situation--which is the ultimate self once the concept of selfhood is fully comprehended. As philosopher T. V. Smith states:

We have now before us perhaps the best answer given by the self-realizational school to the particular question "What desires of what self are to be the moral standard?" The answer is: any desire of any self that can he made compatible with the desires of all selves. And this is made meaningful by the presence of one Self which is inclusive of all selves, being the Eternal Self (Smith and Debbins 1948:80)

Or, as theologian Henry Wellman indicates; "By 'good' I shall mean the experience of being satisfied. This requires something which is satisfying and a self being satisfied. The greatest possible good for any individual is satisfaction of the self in the wholeness of its being and not merely satisfaction at one level which frustrates other levels of the total individuality. Empirical evidence indicates that this kind of satisfaction must be progressive in the sense of expanding more or less continuously the range of what can be appreciated, understood, and controlled by the total unified self; increasing the depth of appreciative understanding which we can have of other individuals; and enlarging the capacity to learn appreciatively from the experience of others across the barrier of diversity and estrangement.

"To distinguish these developments from other kinds, I shall call them collectively the 'creative transformation' of the individual in the wholeness of his being. If creative interchange as above defined produces creative transformation of the individual; then the observation of this consequence is empirical evidence that creative interchange is the greatest good and the saving power in human life" (Wellman 306).

Self-actualization is largely predicated upon a special sense of personal identity which is closely related to certain concepts in Eastern philosophy. Thus, very much as in the original Canons of Buddhism, the growth-motivated person is the person who has overcome the illusion of selfhood as separateness--the need to respond in terms of purely personal needs--and who has managed to merge his personal identity with the larger world around him, perceiving himself as merely a part-function of the whole.

In self-actualization, the individual increasingly comes to comprehend that that which is truly "within" always lies without, that the subjective is inevitably a result of the objective--indeed that mind is ultimately "supraconscious" in the sense that it resides not in personal awareness but rather in the total field of interactive forces which constitute Being-in-general.

Phrased somewhat differently, self-actualization ultimately views the person as a relational nexus and not as a separate entity which can be treated in isolation. It is, in this sense, the world which is "intelligent" and reality which is characterized by "mind" and not merely the person or his society.

The autonomous individual is characteristically less frustrated by reality because he has discovered and realized the necessity of actively cooperating with it. He is more "free" than others tend to be, because he is aware that his nature (including his potentialities for choice) does not exist <u>apart</u> <u>from</u> the natural world hut is <u>continuous</u> <u>with</u> <u>it.</u> He has, already described, integrated his own needs into the basic requirements of the world around him. In so doing, he has redefined his personal needs in such a way as to make them fundamentally compatible with the objective requirements of a larger world.

In a very basic sense, then, the autonomous person is at least implicitly aware of the fundamentally relational structure of all ostensibly centripetal knowledge. Rather than confusing the sort of "selfishness" that Erich Fromm properly distinguishes from true "self-love," he is capable of regarding "the situationally-detached type of knowledge as a marginal and special case of the situationally-determined" (Mannheim 1936:300).

The basic condition for autonomy is a radical intellectual honesty, the requirement to consider all pertinent evidence regardless of where it leads. In a further sense, however, it is to do this, not as a matter of conscious principle, self-consciously holding one's "real" values and interests apart- -but as a matter of preference that grows out of the fact that one has redefined one's real interests to encompass what were previously viewed as the separate interests of others and, indeed, of the encompassing world.

In the autonomous mode of behavior, truth is not a <u>commandment</u> but a <u>passion</u>, and freedom is the product of a fully functioning intelligence. The autonomous person's actions continue to be conditioned by his character, but his character, unlike that of most people, encompasses a larger scope than that circumscribed by narrow ego-needs and unexamined predispositions, and is basically adapted to the objective requirements of a reality that transcends narrow selfhood. To paraphrase Freud, where there was Id, there is now Ego: reality has been assimilated into the pleasure principle.

As pertains to motivation, and as already indicated, the self-actualizing person's behavior continues to be determined by the same basic laws and principles which govern all human behavior. Contrary to what is sometimes suggested in Maslow's terminology, it is not "unmotivated" but merely motivated differently. The growth-motivated person does not grow beyond the necessity of having problems, but the nature and urgency of his problems are distinctively different from those which occur to the deficiency-motivated person. The growth-motivated person retains his individual identity, which is largely the psychological residue of his prior experience. This identity, which the existentialists frequently term "intentionality," continues to exert a strong motivational influence over his behavior. His convictions and concerns are no less intense for being situational and task-centered rather than characterological and self-centered. In self-actualization, the transitive self-as-process takes precedence over the intransitive self-as-product. The self-actualizer is primarily an "I," only secondarily a "me"; far more a "becoming" than a "being."

The chronic gratification of underlying deficiency-needs has led to the sort of situation in which the underlying emotional imperatives of unfinished psychological business--the so-called "hidden agenda" of the deficiency-motivated person--is no longer a significant element in determining the actions of the growth-motivated person. Such an individual seeks the satisfaction of essentially generic biological requirements rather than idiosyncratic psychological demands. This allows him to confront the world on a direct and spontaneous basis largely devoid of the typical emotional static and distortion which interferes with most people's perceptions and cognitions.

On the other hand, such a person is neither unconcerned nor neutral. Quite the contrary, he continues to have strong inclinations and interests, but these tend to operate as preferences which initiate and direct his activities rather than as compulsions and constraints which force his behavior into rigidly predetermined patterns of response.

In a sense, it is this emotional flexibility that provides the growth-motivated person with the capacity for creative self-transcendence. His diffuse commitment to a wide-variety of possibilities for action gives him the capacity to adapt his inclinations to the requirements of the situation-at-hand and to re-channel his interests and directions more congruent with the objective conditions that exist. His behavior is "situationally-congruous" in the fullest sense of the term. Since he is able to adapt his own requirements to those of the situation with which he is confronted, he is capable of participating in the meaning inherent within the situation rather than forcing the situation to satisfy his own prepotent emotional needs. "Playful" in the best sense of the word, he is capable not only of "playing the game" effectively but even of altering the game to be played--the way the situation is perceived and comprehended--so that it better suits the circumstances that prevail.

Self-actualization, like all behavior, is "motivated" by tensions that demand tension- reduction. The tensions that underlie self-actualization are at basis teleological, for subjective potentialities can be expressed only in terms of objective (ontological) possibilities that must be adapted to the requirements of internal needs. A <u>potentiality</u> is, then, always at basis a structure-function and, as Erik Erikson has said, the "newer concepts of environment (such as the <u>Umwelt</u> of the Ethologists) imply an optimum relation of inborn potentialities and the structure of the environment" (Erikson 1994:3).

Ironically the fullest development of autonomous behavior probably leads away from explicitly cognitive reason and becomes much more "intuitive." This is true for a variety of reasons--because the problems of autonomous people tend to become more subtle and less amenable to purely "rational" solutions over a period of time, because they discover less need for explicit clarity and accuracy, and so on. The basic reason, however, is that the autonomous person gradually becomes "aware" that the reason inherent <u>within</u> his behavior is frequently superior to the reason he imposes <u>upon</u> his behavior.

Phrased somewhat differently, he frequently discovers that he can be more reasonable with <u>less</u> reasoning, that the cumbersome process of translating his behavior into symbols and relating these vicariously by means of cognition is either inefficient because it is too cumbersome and time-consuming to be superior to "impulsive" decisions or because it actually keeps him from being fully available to many of the nonverbal cues and relevant non-symbolic feelings that are also pertinent to the question at hand and that might make a significant contribution to the best solution. The way in which this occurs could be outlined as follows:

As thought becomes more fully autonomous, then, it becomes characteristically less and less critical, increasingly "esthetic." More and more, there is a congruency between thought and feeling. Directed by a less self-consciously and conventional "rational" set of responses, the individual's thought processes become increasingly directed by the objective requirements, the natural flow and rhythm, of the situation itself. Feelings, intimations, "intuitions" become increasingly more significant, and the motor-emotional antecedents of rational behavior attain a new centrality. In the more advanced phases of autonomous thought, a new and "higher" form of <u>participational</u> <u>intelligence</u> evolves in which subject and object collaborate in a mute creative dialectic in which even the traditional divisions between and matter become vague and difficult to define. In some cases, life becomes (as French philosopher Gabriel Marcel once remarked) a mystery to be lived and not a problem to be solved. The idea is suggested by Camus in the following words:

"To lick ones life like a stick of barley sugar, to form, sharpen, and finally fall in love with it, in the same way as one searches for the word, the image, the definitive sentence, the word or image which marks a close or conclusion, from which one can start out again, and which will color the way we see the world" (Camus 1965:58).

With respect to actual "intuitive" choices, the autonomous person, like any other, is likely to be "probability-programmed." Obviously, this does not mean that he performs mathematical computations to derive the likelihood that one choice is better than another in a purely arithmetical sense. It does mean that he probably automatically assesses the subjective value of perceived options by comparing the motor-emotional (pleasure-pain) impact of the anticipated options. Each in turn elicits a subliminal motor-emotional response associated with performing the same or similar actions in relevant situations in the past. The idea which elicits the greatest positive emotional response on a tacit basis is acted upon first, and so on, in a rough rank-order of pre-rational preferences. The whole process would seem to involve a sort of instantaneous and unconscious calculus that is based upon some sort of genetic algorhythm.

In all likelihood, a combination of approach-avoidance tendencies are aroused and interact to give rise to each particular pre-perceptual response-set In a sense, then, intuitive responses are based upon an objective (hedonic) "logic of assent." The impulsive behavior of the autonomous person is more trustworthy than that of the deficiency- motivated person because his behavior has been more efficient and his emotional impulses are therefore tacitly reasonable. His "feelings" are intelligent on an after-the-fact basis.

As self-actualizing behavior is continuously confirmed and strengthened synergistically through its own positive consequences, the habits developed out of the circular and self-confirming behavior become increasingly stronger, and the ideational aspects--the thinking about what one is doing--becomes less and less significant as a source of action. Effective behavior as such tends to become more or less automatic and habitual.

9. Autonomy III

Human beings have the capacity to comprehend the limits and conditions that control their own behavior. It is precisely this understanding which provides them with a margin of control--a "finite freedom"--over those very limits and conditions. As Ralph Barton Perry states: "The power of man to shape his cosmic destiny is pitifully small, but in principle it is unlimited. For in proportion as man knows what these limits are, and what are their causes, the way is open to remove them, by indirection, by organization, and by playing one natural force against another." (Perry 1954:462).

As philosopher Abraham Kaplan puts it:

"Man is free when his choices are the product of full awareness of operative needs and actual constraints.... To know what he truly wants and what he can truly have--this truth does not make man free, but makes freedom possible. Self-mastery is not antecedently guaranteed, but is something to be achieved.

"This conception of freedom accords well with the Stoics formula of 'recognition of necessity,' Spinoza's 'determination by reason,' and Dewey's 'reflective choice'" (Kaplan 1963:139).

The way in which autonomous behavior evolves out of self-actualization can be outlined roughly as follows:

126

Effective behavior in the developmental years is essentially precognitive and yet implicitly "reasonable" behavior in the sense that it serves to resolve tensions and to generate pleasure in the same way that subsequent "reasoned" behavior will do.

Constancies and continuities within such precognitive reinforced behavior are retained in memory and, are ultimately transformed symbolically into abstract representations of such similarities that are internalized to form the basis of the emerging self-system and the beginning of subjective volition.

Through this process "reasoned" behavior emerges out of tacitly "reasonable" behavior. The child develops his "reason" in three senses:

1) He interiorizes a host of objective beliefs. These are initially beliefs about the hedonic potential of various objects and events but evolve in time into more general beliefs about the nature and characteristics of the world in general.
2) As he matures, he develops beliefs with respect to the "rules" (such as cause-and-effect) which order behavior and, ultimately, of the laws of logic which are secondary rules that govern the processes of communicating about such behavior.
3) At a still later phase of development, he masters and interiorizes particular ways of conducting intellectual inquiry that help him to perceive problems objectively and to solve problems effectively.

Other things being equal, the child who passes successfully through the need-gratification cycle in the earliest years of life emerges as an adult who can be characterized in the following ways:

1) He subscribes, consciously or unconsciously, to the empirical premise which holds that all knowledge is the product of personal experience and that there is no such things as metaphysical (or absolute) knowledge.
2) He accepts the notion that all experience is the product of personal behavior in the natural (sense-perceptual) world.

3) He subscribes to the point of view (albeit at third remove and inferentially) of philosophical realism, holding that, while there is no direct and certain knowledge, there is nevertheless a factual world that is put together in a particular way which ultimately governs behavior and therefore generates a particular kind of consciousness, as well as a particular type of knowledge, rather than another.

Phrased somewhat differently, such a person comes to understand that we know the world refracted through our own subjective experience, . which is shaped by our own personal behavior. This behavior is, in turn, relative to particular situations in the real (impersonal) world. On the other hand, situationality--the conditions that govern the world in general not relative at all but is objectively predetermined and can be comprehended through the proper pursuit of knowledge, utilizing scientific problem-solving procedures and common sense adaptations of such procedures such as those presented in such philosophical orientations as pragmatism and experimentalism.

All of these characteristics of self-actualizing thought--empiricism defined in terms of behaviorism, qualified realism, experimentalism (which is based on pragmatism and which encompasses traditional scientific problem-solving procedures in its most rigorous expression) work to advance effective behavior, because they are factual (objective) descriptions of the nature and content of human experience. They are the preeminent means-values which contribute to all more specific end-values. As the individual grows older, this multifaceted reason gradually assumes the status of a secondary reinforcer, and it is transformed from the cognitive to the normative--to the status of an end-value as well as a system of beliefs. The individual slowly begins to grasp that his most central value is not the value of this or that but, rather, the value of a particular self-orientation based on a belief-system and on ways of thinking about the world which have a general value that transcends all particular values whatsoever and even provides the overriding means to the realization of all other values. In a sense, he has found the conceptual equivalent of the "philosopher's stone" which is no less than a way of knowing and being that is founded upon an ontology forged within the parameters of a particular psychology.

Through the process of intellectual abstraction such a person has arrived at the normative apex of the cognitive, the view that overriding value resides primarily in a passionate commitment to a particular sort of knowing--the pursuit of objective knowledge, viewed as a prepotent categorical need that takes precedence over all more particular needs and that is synergistically interwoven with his entire pattern of progressively more satisfactory ongoing experience as this transpires within the process of self-actualization.

In such a way, the autonomous individual has resolved one of the fundamental dichotomies within traditional philosophy, the dichotomy between truth and value. In the case of autonomy, truth, both in its substantive and procedural aspects, evolves developmentally out of value (that is, the ultimate biological value is pleasure, and we learn through the instrumentality of pleasure), but, once an objective representation of truth has emerged, it becomes the central value, because it is, in effect, the regulating means-value which guarantees the fullest realization of all particular goals and which guarantees the maximum realization of pleasure by providing a definitive vision of "happiness" that ultimately brings both means and ends into convergence in an ongoing cycle of positive synergistic behavior. In such cases, "isness" becomes "oughtness," and the usual tension between the two ostensible antinomies has become effectively resolved.

In a similar sense, the traditional dichotomy of self and other, self and non-self, is also resolved in the case of autonomy, because truth is viewed as interpersonal and universal by definition. Clearly conceived any full understanding of self-actualization entails an understanding that others are inextricable aspects of the self, fully conceived, and the differences between self and other, self and non-self, are recognized to be essentially semantic differences in the light of an overriding objective consciousness. In a similar sense, since consciousness is bipolar--as fully contingent upon the objective world as on the subjective self--there can be no full comprehension of <u>self</u> without an equally compelling attention to the "impersonal" aspects of being.

The autonomous person's overriding commitment to objective knowledge generates a fuller comprehension of reality-as-it-is, thereby making the world more <u>intelligible</u>, and, since there is a necessary complimentarity between <u>intelligibility</u> and personal intelligence, making the individual and his society correspondingly more <u>intelligent.</u>

In this way, autonomy contributes both to personal and social self-actualization-- which, through an inexorable sort of feedback loop--also augments autonomy. All of this ensures a positive synergism cycle, a self-perpetuating heurism that pervades all the processes of cognition, conation and affect.

As autonomous behavior develops it is reinforced by its own effective consequences and therefore becomes self-reinforcing in a positive direction. It becomes less random, and, because effective behavior is demonstrably rational, it tends to be less egocentric (that is, <u>subjective</u> in the usual sense of the term) as wall as less arbitrary.

Volition is increasingly consolidated and strengthened on a rational level through the consequences of natural reinforcement and, in time, the individual spontaneously seeks to do that which is most "objectively" intelligent. His behavior becomes increasingly efficient, more or less objectively rational but on an after-the-fact, subjective (motor- emotional) basis. Behavior becomes increasingly mediated by impulses and feelings which have been verified as objectively rational through the verifying (hedonic) consequences of past behavior. This frees the individual to attend consciously (rationally) to new and important problems and also allows him to attend more closely to the pre-perceptual (nonverbal, configurational, emotional, "unconscious") and perceptual (informational) aspects of situations which are either noncognitive or less directly cognitive in nature. This provides him with better and more complete input-- better problem-perception--and further confirms the accuracy of impulsive and/or intuitive responses mediated by tacit cues and other inarticulable factors.

This, in turn, allows the autonomous person who seeks an accurate reality-orientation to have fuller access to reality as a basis for action. It allows him to get even further <u>outside</u> of himself and hence to correct mistaken assumptions and to formulate new impressions less bound by his established cognitive preconceptions. This increases his openness to experience and augments his capacity to "get with" the situation at hand. It also enhances the accuracy and relevance of his problem-perception and makes his responses (both behavioral and symbolic) more truly cogent to the circumstances at hand. The entire process is fundamentally heuristic in two senses: (1) self-actualization gives rise to autonomy and autonomy, once established, confirms and strengthens self-actualization.

Self-actualization and Autonomy
Self-actualizing behavior (objective behavior)
    gives rise to
objective goals and values
    which eventuate in
objective problem-perceiving
    which is a necessary precondition for
objective problem-solving
    which gives rise to
pleasure
    which causes learning,
    which terminates in the sort of
knowledge
    which produces
more self-actualizing (objective) behavior,
    and which may ultimately eventuate in
autonomy

Self-actualizing people tend to be capable of autonomy, because they have learned the value of reasoned behavior naturally as an outgrowth of rational self-development. In self-actualization the self as <u>product</u>--beliefs, values, personal identity, and so on--is normally an outgrowth of the self as <u>process</u>-- reasonable behavior directed to reasonable (objectively-perceived) problems.

The self-actualizing person is an "I" before he is a "me." His beliefs are a product of his experience which is, in turn, a product of long-term effective behavior, grounded in the natural dialectic of objective cause-and-effect relationships.

The self-actualizing person is autonomous not merely because he understands himself, but because the self he understands is fundamentally reasonable, representing an internalized vision of previous encounters with the world-as-it-is. He is able to transcend himself, because his selfhood is based upon principles of action which apply to the world in general, including his own nature. He is guided by the internalized principles of reason which initially emerged from and therefore properly characterize the natural world as such. He is self-transcending, because he presents what Sidney Jourard has called a "transparent self," because his essential selfhood is focused on principles which are essentially impersonal and applicable to reality in general. In this sense, he responds to the rhythms of a larger self and is capable of changing in and through this heightened sensitivity. He becomes what he <u>experiences</u>, but he experiences through what he <u>is</u>, and what he is--his basic identity--is, in turn, determined by an overriding commitment to becoming what is possible through the passionate pursuit of objective understanding.

The traditional dichotomy between "isness" and "oughtness" is misleading, because the conventional line of reasoning has assumed that isness precedes and should therefore determine oughtness. In point of fact, however, the contrary is closer to the truth; value precedes and determines truth. The first things that the individual experiences are the proto-values of pleasure-pain. What he experiences in the world and subsequently comes to desire is determined primarily by the hedonic consequences of his own behavior in the earliest stages of life. Pleasure remains the sole psychological value, and happiness is merely a way of configuring pleasure and pain over time and through space.

If anything, the self-actualizing person has a heightened sense of self--he knows who he is and what he believes in--but this "self" is essentially objective and therefore "selfless" in the sense that it is founded upon profoundly reasonable (and therefore objectively testable) principles for determining action and for verifying belief.

Contrary to much opinion, the person with a weak sense of self is not more "open to his environment," he is merely less discriminating in his responses. He is certainly no more "objective," because "objectivity" is a passion for a particular type of knowledge and not a lack of conviction and concern. "A man without passions," Helvetius once noted, "is incapable of that degree of attention to which a superior judgment is annexed: a superiority that is perhaps less the effect of an extraordinary effort than an habitual attention" (Bruner 1963:24). "What is the use of knowing? asks the Devil in Shaw's Man and Superman. 'Why,' responds Don Juan, 'to be able to choose the line of greatest advantage instead of yielding in the direction of the least resistance. Does a ship sail to its destination no better than a log drifts nowhither? The philosopher is Nature's pilot. And there you have our difference: to be in hell is to drift: to be in heaven is to steer'" (Shaw 141).

In self-actualization there is such a thing as "objective truth," but it can only be apprehended indirectly. The line of reasoning might be outlined as follows:

We only know our own personal experience (subjective phenomena).
Personal experience consists of covert (psychological) responses to overt behavioral responses that are elicited by the interaction between the organism and its environment
Subjectivity emerges out of psychological responses to more fundamental physical responses.
Therefore reality is basically physical (objective), but it is apprehended psychologically (subjectively).

Where psychological responses are essentially non-refractive, as in the case of growth-motivated perception, the individual adapts his needs to the requirements of the situation so that a disproportionate number of his needs tend to be satisfied and therefore reinforced (as compared to the average non-self-actualizing person). The same or similar situations tend to evoke the same or similar need-gratification sequences within personal behavior.

In the case of self-actualization, as cognition matures the understandings and values that emerge from these established sequences of need-gratifications are internalized as objective meanings--true ideas about the nature and relevance of various sorts of situations as these relate to the "objective consciousness" of the self-actualizing person.

This leads to two different types of objective meaning: (1) the individual comes to understand his own needs and values, and (2) the individual comes to understand the essential meaning of his own cumulative knowledge realized through growth-motivated objective cognition in response to the world-as-it-is.

This basic understanding of self and world provides the necessary substratum of sanity that terminates in an <u>objective subjectivity</u> where the individual's fundamental motive is to see things as they are in the absence of the usual sort of prepotent motivational distortions.

As the individual evolves out of deficiency-motivation, he moves naturally in the direction of intellectual commitment (a sort of pervasive intellectual curiosity which serves as an overriding need-orientation) because of the natural superiority of such an orientation as a basis for generating a consistent sequence of positive emotional experience. He experiences "happiness" not as an abstract theory but as a mode of interacting with the world.

Such characteristic happiness provides the affective and cognitive basis for the emergence of a fully functioning self-actualization. In this sense, happiness generates truth (both perceptually as process and cognitively as product), and truth, in turn, generates additional happiness.

This fusion of cognition, conation and affect leads progressively to an ego- identification with others as an aspect of self (altruistic love), to an ego-generalization with more encompassing aspects of the world beyond the purely social ("objective love") and, on occasion, to an overriding and prepotent commitment to truth-as-a-value (autonomy).

In this way, knowledge evolves into wisdom--the utilization of knowledge to create and sustain happiness--and the entire process becomes continuous, interconfirming and heuristic.

The Evolution of Personal Autonomy

Positive hedonic consequences of personal behavior
Initial goals (knowledge of particular ends-values)
Initial values (knowledge of abstract ends-values)
Formative understanding of truth (know of information and procedures utilized as overall means-values)
Perceptual and cognitive objectivity
Positive synergy
Meta-value of autonomy (commitment to perceptual and cognitive objectivity as an operational definition of self-actualization)
Advancement of positive synergy: the augmentation and perfection of self-actualization through the modality of autonomy.

10. Typology I

Viewed from the empirical-naturalist point of view, which sees pleasure as the ultimate psychological value and happiness as the ultimate means-value for optimizing pleasure in the long run or on balance, there are four basic ways of attempting to realize personal happiness. These differ primarily in how they relate to two fundamental variables: (1) functional intelligence and (2) personal commitment

The term *intelligence* is ambiguous at best. In the basic sense, however, there are two fundamental views of *intelligence*: (1) *intelligence* as the potential capacity for solving problems effectively and (2) intelligence as the actual ability to solve problems effectively. In this sense, many people with the potential capacity for effective problem solving do not exhibit much of an actual ability to do so.

Closely associated with this distinction, is the related difference between the (essentially cognitive) capacity to solve problems and the (equally cognitive but ordinarily more characterological) capacity to perceive problems (or, from the point of view of self-actualization theory, to perceive problems objectively by responding to situations "as-they-are"). What sets the self-actualizing individual apart from most others is, as Maslow notes, the fact that he has a significant intellectual capacity (for symbolism, reason, and related intellectual processes) which is attuned to an objective recognition of the world-as-it-is. This, in turn, eventuates in a markedly heightened capacity for solving real problems. Such a person's intelligence is *functional intelligence* because it represents a fusion of intellectual capacity and perceptual objectivity that yields a high degree of actual "problem solving ability" in the broadest sense of the term.

Functional intelligence is essentially a process of effective problem solving. On the other hand, it also and necessarily yields a *product--*knowledgeability--which consists of a person's capacity to recall prior experiences and, perhaps even more important, to derive generalized interpretations (meanings) from such experiences which can be used as effective tools in future problem solving. Fully functioning intelligence encompasses problem solving abilities which combine the *process* of thinking with the *product* of prior thinking (in the form of memories, ideas and various psychological associations). These come together to form a continuous and heuristic sort of cognitive involvement between self and situation.

Personal commitment is closely related to the more general idea of *motivation*. It is, however, a more focused concept than "motivation" as such. *Personal commitment* is motivation directed toward some defined course of action. It is, in this sense, a sort of "achievement motivation," because the individual pursues a course of action that is intended to eventuate in some sort of long-term accomplishment, which may envision virtually anything from writing the great American novel to pursuing the social goal of universal literacy.

In this sense, personal commitment always implies some generalized course of action which encompasses a number of more specific goal sequences over a prolonged period of time. Such a commitment may not directly affect other people. It may be directed almost entirely toward the pursuit of theoretical knowledge in an area like astronomy or particle physics that is not ordinarily viewed as a social enterprise. On the other hand, since man is naturally social, and by logical extension, moral, any personal commitment is also a sort of social and moral commitment, as well. Any choice of self is, in this sense, necessarily an indirect choice of (and for) others.

With these considerations in mind, it is possible to come up with a schemata which presents four basic models that feature different combinations of personal commitment and functional intelligence. These might be labeled low commitment/low intellectualism, low commitment/ high intellectualism, high commitment/low intellectualism, and high commitment/high intellectualism.

Like all typologies, this one can be expressed in a variety of different ways. Factors can be broken down into subfactors to produce not four but eight, sixteen, thirty-two, or even more different subfactors. In the present instance, there are two substantially different expressions of personal commitment--personal commitment (which also entails a type of social commitment), on the one hand, and ontological commitment (that is, commitment to objective truth as a subjective value) on the other hand, and since there are also two substantially different aspects to what is described as "intellectualism" intellectual ability (what is ordinarily viewed as "intelligence"), on the one hand, and breadth and depth of knowledgeability, on the other--it could be argued that there are actually sixteen basic response-sets, ranging from all "high" to all "low" on four different factors in various combinations. If one were to differentiate between subjective (metaphysical) and objective (empirical naturalist) worldviews, it would be possible to design a model with six different factors replete with all of the various combinations. Even more complicated scenarios can be imagined. This model is meant to be suggestive rather than exhaustive.

This picture is also complicated by the fact that each of the four response-sets can operate on the bans of a philosophical/religious worldview that is either naturalistic in the sense that it is rooted in basic assumptions that are essentially restricted in natural experience, postulating a world that is ultimately reducible to personal experience based upon behavioral interactions between the physical organism and the physical environment, or is *supernaturalistic* in the sense that it is based upon assumptions that postulate a world that is, in some significant sense, based upon the interaction between an organism or environment (or both) which in some central respect transcends the physical laws of the purely natural world and therefore exists on a supernaturalistic or metaphysical basis.

Since the model of self-actualization presented here constitutes a "soft-behaviorism" that is based upon a philosophical point of view which is perhaps best described as "empirical naturalism," it holds, in part, that supernaturalistic and metaphysical systems of belief, which maintain that some realm of being exists beyond the natural/physical are necessarily "subjective" in the sense that they distort the real (natural) nature of the world and, in so doing, also warp the individual's capacity to perceive the world "as-it--is" and to deal with it on a "realistic" basis. In Figure 1--the low commitment/low intellectualism response-set--for example, where the individual exhibits a markedly low degree of functional intelligence in combination with an equally low intensity of personal commitment-- such a person would assumedly even more markedly low-low if he were philosophically or religiously "subjective" than he would be if he subscribed to an empirical naturalistic view of the world, because his psychological subjectivism would be compounded and reinforced by an equally subjective (anti-naturalistic) worldview.

Low Commitment/Low Intellectualism

This type presents perhaps the most dismal picture of the four types of personal orientation, because here the individual combines a low level of functional intelligence with a low level of personal commitment. This tends to block any sort of significant involvement and therefore reduces the potential intensity of pleasurable experience. Such a person perceives less meaning from his encounters in the world and, as a result, has a comparatively rudimentary understanding of it. He confronts his significant problems. At basis, he experiences less of the world and he experiences this with diminished intensity. Such a person is biologically alive, but he is only marginally alive in a psychological sense. He is, in common parlance, both stupid and indifferent.

Such an orientation may be determined by nature (temperament, energy level, innate intellectual capacities, or such), nurture, or (more commonly) by both. In the absence of biological (including neurological) defects, such an orientation is probably most often the result of motor-emotional conditioning during infancy and early childhood. The individual has been taught to anticipate failure and frustration from taking the initiative--from "being active"--as well as from trying to resolve problems cognitively. He learns to live defensively, by subduing his emotions and by avoiding intellectual responses to problems whenever possible, becoming essentially *nonintellectual* or (in some cases) *anti-intellectual* in his encounters with new experiences.

Such a person is as free to act as anyone else, but he refuses to exercise this freedom, in effect "choosing not to choose." In so doing, he becomes a more or less passive victim of circumstances.

Assuming that such a person is not neurologically handicapped or otherwise impaired and that he is therefore capable of functioning differently, he has, in effect, opted for a mode of behavior/experience in which he chooses to think as little as possible--to reduce his cognitive involvement to as low a level as possible--to think as superficially as he can, restricting his cognition, in so far as possible, to the relatively unreflective realm of simple perceptual orientation, thinking only about those things that have been subceptually assessed to be more or less innocuous. Such a person has, in effect, committed "psychological suicide"--responding slowly, superficially, and at the most muted level possible to the surrounding world. He has effectively managed to restrict his behavior to a minimum and, correspondingly, to reduce his consciousness to match his minimized psychological involvement.

Such a passive pattern of behavior, which the existentialists tend to view as one form of what they call "bad faith," is essentially a pathology of deficiency and frustration. Such a person has characteristically been conditioned to anticipate frustration and defeat from virtually any kind of response, and his entire life has become a sustained sequence of "sins of omission." Anticipating failure from action, he has learned to avoid as much significant action as possible in order to minimize his losses. Frequently this orientation is augmented by drugs, like alcohol, that are essentially depressive in their effects, slowing reaction and otherwise subduing cognitive awareness of surrounding conditions. For such a person, life has become primarily an escape from reality through a course of action (or inaction) which is, at best, a sort of self-abnegation.

Low Commitment/High Intellectualism

This type presents the somewhat less depressing prospect of the low-high configuration. Here there is a low degree of personal commitment but a high degree of functional intelligence. Such a person is characteristically intelligent in the sense that he perceives many problems and that he can deal with them both quickly and effectively. On the other hand, he has little emotional investment in any particular course of action, so the tension-reduction generated by his cognition elicits only a marginal degree of pleasure. Such a person may be cognitively effective but he remains affectively flat. His emotional life is muted by a lack of serious commitment; he is bright but indifferent.

Again, assuming no significant neurological defects, such a personal orientation is also probably the consequence of defective child-rearing, where the child has learned through the emotional feedback from his own behavior that heavy emotional investments are likely to result in frustration and failure. His response is to become an intellectual voyeur rather than an active participant in the world around him.

High Commitment/Low Intellectualism

This type presents the contrary of the second type. This is the *high-low* configuration, which combines a high degree of emotional commitment with a low degree of functional intelligence. Such a person is intensely committed to some course of action, but he exhibits a low degree of functional intelligence. He attains a great deal of emotional gratification from what he does, but he comprehends few relevant opportunities for action. He is passionate but not very bright.

Whether this orientation is more or less "positive' than the second type is debatable. It seems that a more effective cognition, which generates better information, might conceivably provide more promise for positive potential change in the area of increased emotional involvement than the opposite situation which is characterized by a heightened achievement motivation in combination with low functional intelligence, but neither of the two scenarios seems to be particularly promising.

The non-intellectual orientations--the low commitment/low intellectualism model and the high commitment/low intellectualism model can be expressed as either the *opposite* of intellectualism (the tendency not to think, to avoid cognitive encounters with the world), or its *contrary* (the tendency to reject the rational procedures and/or empirical assumptions, such as cause-and-effect determinism) that are necessary for valid and objective thinking. (In some instances, such orientations may be expressed as combinations of both of these.) The distinction is potentially very significant, but it clearly goes beyond the scope of this very preliminary sketch of what is a potentially exceedingly complicated topic. For present purposes the term "nonintellectual" is used to cover both *nonintellectual* and *anti-intellectual* approaches as well as mixtures of the two.

Such a person is perhaps best represented by some fervently religious individuals who adhere to a literalistic interpretation of scripture. In contrast to the low commitment/low-intellectualism person who seeks to avoid choice, this kind of person actively involves himself in the sort of life-orientation that might be better described as active false-consciousness (what the existentialists tend to view as "active bad faith") in the sense that it calls for constructing and maintaining a commitment to an alternative, subjective reality-orientation that defines substantial aspects of the real (empirical naturalistic) world into metaphysical/supernaturalistic terms that misrepresent the real nature of the world as-it-is.

Such a person is not "insane" in the sense of being psychotic (as in schizophrenia) because it appears increasingly probable that the so-called "psychotic" disorders probably stem primarily from neurological defects that are principally genetic in origin and that alter the very nature and quality of what presents itself as ostensibly objective personal experience, giving rise to a surrogate reality that generates substantially different patterns of behavior than what occurs in those who are not so afflicted.

Mark Twain is famous for posing the moral conundrum in which God confronts a person with the question "If I could promise you total happiness upon the single condition that you would also be totally insane, would you accept?"

The choice is fascinating, but from the point of view of the empirical naturalist, such an option would be difficult for even God to make available because, short of redefining reality altogether, human happiness is unavoidably contingent upon the highest development of objective reason- -which would preclude the possibility of "insane happiness" altogether. In the world as it exists, insanity would necessarily lead to ineffective behavior, which would unavoidably work against the individual's survival and success within the world as it is and therefore preclude the possibility of true "happiness."

If God were to rephrase the proposal by saying, in effect, "I will guarantee you total happiness on the single condition that you will be totally insane in a substantially different kind of world in which insanity guarantees the sort of affective experience that is produced out of the most effective behavior possible within the world as you presently know it-- saying, in essence, "I would create the kind of insane world in which your insane behavior would be reinforced a person would have to be "mad" to reject the proposition.

The whole point of *sanity* is to insure *happiness*. To reject happiness in favor of sanity--in circumstances where sanity would defeat the possibility of happiness--would be "insanity."

This third type functions in substantially in the same way as a neurosis. The individual's behavior/experience is significantly defective and is characterized by a high level of frustration and psychic pain. For any of a number of reasons, he finds that objective reality does not address his psychological needs, so he progressively distorts reality so that it will be invested with a meaning more compatible with his more imperative subjective requirements.

In a similar sense, in the case of conventional, supernaturalistic religion, the individual yields to a predefined alternative reality that is more congenial to his subjective responses than the world as-it-is. Such a person buys into an "institutionalized neurosis" that is pre-established and therefore ready for adoption rather than being forced to create a defensive personal delusion. In so doing, certain significant beliefs and values central to this subjective orientation become prepotent over their objective counterparts and begin to cognitively prevail and to become directive in the individual's life.

In this way, a negative synergism cycle comes to prevail in the individual's life, and, as in the case of deficiency-motivated perception, the consequences of cognitive distortion reinforce this supernaturalistic (and therefore empirically "unrealistic") belief-system in an immediate sense and also generate the long-term need for even more extensive sorts of self-delusion in the future.

Whether and to what extent social neuroses, like fervent religious commitments of the usual sort, are reinforced, depends on many factors in addition to psychological susceptibility and the social availability of such belief-systems in the first place. The social acceptability of such orientations is, of course, of primary importance, and, in this respect, there tend to be four types of cultures:

a) Those cultures which reward what the secular world looks upon as a sort of "religious insanity," viewing it as providing an entree into a higher type of "supernatural" reality-orientation.

b) Those cultures where conventional religion is socially sanctioned and reinforced, as in most cultures where there is no separation of church and state, and where some prescribed type and degree of religiosity is viewed as a normal component of "sanity" as socially defined.

c) Those cultures where conventional religious views are tolerated but only marginally reinforced, and where the dominant social ideology does not incorporate a particular religious orientation as a necessary aspect of sanity as socially defined.

d) Those cultures where conventional religion is looked upon as essentially aberrant behavior, viewed essentially as a sort of institutionalized neurosis of the sort that Marx once referred to as "the opium of the people."

The Communist Party as it existed in the Soviet Union and in China during the third quarter of the twentieth century, or, in a drastically different direction, the "objectivist" philosophy of Ayn Rand--while ostensibly naturalistic and objective, are actually metaphysical and subjectivistic when subjected to close scrutiny. In the case of Communism, for example, Marx's rephrasing of Hegel's dialectic assumes that an objective and positive synergism operates in the natural world. The *synthesis* that emerges from the conflict between the *thesis* and the *antithesis* is always superior to both the thesis and the antithesis out of which it emerged, so the world is getting demonstrably better and better as time goes by. The Communists also assumed that history was capable of being construed "scientifically" by a sort of reverse verification based upon "objective" ideological analysis. These are plausible notions, but dubious for a variety of reasons.

On the other hand, the overall Communist point of view is so all-informing and totalistic (in the sense that it provides an in-system explanation for virtually any question that may occur) that it becomes an ideologically self-verifying closed-system which eliminates the possibility of correction on the basis of credible, disconfirming evidence. In essence, there are no fundamental problems in such a closed-system, because all such problems are implicitly answered by the system itself. As in the case of personal neurosis, the pathology creates an even greater reliance on the controlling symptomatology until the symptomatology becomes so disabling that the entire system collapses of its own weight, and the need for a new way of thinking and acting becomes undeniable.

The major problem with organized, external subjectifications of the world, whether these stem from organized conventional religion or organized political religion like Communism can be reduced in two basic points. First, such subjectification can never be actually *totally* short of psychosis, because even where closed and absolute systems of belief are readily available, they coexist with the real-world of material objects and events that elicit a significant degree of realistic behavior (and therefore realistic belief) which is implicitly opposed to metaphysical and supernaturalistic worldviews. The child experiences pleasure; he generalizes pleasurable objects and events into his first goals; and he abstracts these goals into a formative set of values *before* he comprehends the world cognitively.

In this sense, ideological indoctrination is always largely a matter of counter-indoctrination that aims to promote the active reinterpretation of experience that has already evolved out of the earliest months and years of motor-emotional conditioning in response to pre-ideational adaptations to real situations that predate subjectivity itself. The initial self-system that emerges out of the earliest behavior, is, in this sense, essentially non-ideological. Subsequent attempts to redefine this self-system on a symbolic level in metaphysical terms are never totally satisfactory because this refractory set of tacit understandings which are motor-emotional in nature and which precede more sophisticated but counter-intuitive ideological worldviews.

Secondly, in this sense, all supernaturalistic education is a matter of re-education, and the conflict between the precognitive, intuitive learning that gives rise to the earliest cognitive comprehension of the world, on the one hand, and the cognitive restructuring of the earliest assumptions through subsequent ideological re-education based on supernaturalistic or metaphysical principles is never fully successful.

In most cases subjective belief-systems are propagated vicariously through words and verbal reasoning. Many of these concepts are tacitly opposed to already established empirical assumptions that have emerged out of previous motor-emotional conditioning: The notion that one should be self-sacrificing at a time when selfhood (personal identity) itself has only partially evolved creates feelings of ambivalence and ambiguity. In a similar sense, the introduction of abstract concepts that are not grounded in previous experience and that frequently seem to be tacitly opposed to such experience because they do not seem coherent within it--concepts like heaven, hell, soul, immortality, and such--creates a sense of profound intellectual conflict in most children.

Such ideas not only violate objective, common sense experience. They also force children to generate misconceptions as a way of attempting to comprehend the irrational. They are forced to rationalize the irrational, and, further, to do so on the basis of immature cognitive processes, long before their potential for reason and for reasoned imagination have matured sufficiently to make such an undertaking possible. In most cases, the ideas formulated remain vague, amorphous and ambiguous--infantile misconceptions which are brought to bear as controlling ontological absolutes on a more or less continuing basis as the child matures.

This subjectification of reality not only distracts children from the gratification of their emerging biological and psychological needs. It also distorts the way they perceive these needs and thereby blocks their fullest realization.

The subjectivity that emerges from such misrepresentations of reality subverts true objectivity. It leads to all of the deteriorating behaviors which, in the long run, generate and serve to intensify the frustration/distortion cycle of negative behavior so characteristic of deficiency-motivated people. Such subjectivity not only blocks autonomy, but creativity as well, for any total and self-confirming system of thought already contains the answers to all of life's most central questions. Such ideology is programmatic and not merely procedural; it encompasses both problem-perceiving and problem-solving as they relate to all of the truly central questions about the human condition. Significant new answers are irrelevant where there are no significant new questions or where a preexisting interpretive context envelops and stifles all serious critical inquiry.

Ironically, the solution to engrained subjectivity is not objectivity, because, in the mythology of conventional religion, objective understandings are looked upon as false and therefore evil. Evoking objective concepts to confront subjective misunderstandings tends to merely heighten anxiety in subjective people and therefore to reinforce the emotional climate necessary to strengthen their neurotic defenses. Any conversion back to the objective must be gradual and indirect, not attempted by means of ideological combat. Someone who believes in special creation is unlikely to be converted by a discourse on Darwin.

These comments assume that we are dealing with subjectivity within an overriding context of sanity and not with the more or less self-contained subjectivity characteristic of the psychotic, which is a substantially different question.

Other things being equal, a subjective reality-orientation is less effective than an objective one for three basic reasons:

1) Subjectivity is, by definition, a partial denial (suppression/repression) of objective consciousness. It causes the individual to misrepresent the meaning of the situation as-it-is in order to satisfy prepotent biological and psychological

needs. In the long run, such an orientation exacerbates a person's predisposition toward perceptual inaccuracy and chronic behavioral ineffectiveness, augmenting an already self-confirming cycle of negatively synergistic behavior.

2) In most cases, subjectivity militates against effective personal commitment because it creates ambiguity and conflict between the naturalistic worldview that emerges normally out of trial-and-error behavior and its supernaturalistic counterpart. In conventional religion, for example, most significant acts have both a natural meaning and significance and a supernatural meaning and significance, and the two are often in substantial variance. As a consequence, the question of how to perceive a situation is frequently sufficiently problematic to substantially delay the subsequent behavioral responses involved in problem-solving.

All cognition, including perception, is affective, but the level of affect is ordinarily more elevated in the case of *applied* cognition, where thought is used to bring about actual changes in the real world.

Thought is essentially vicarious experience. Vicarious experience, while it also involves tacit felt-thought on the motor-muscular level, involves a lesser intensity of emotional response when it is not directed toward the real world of actual objects and events.

This is true because the organism is tacitly aware that it is behaving in reaction to internal (electro-chemical) responses within the central nervous system that are directed *volitionally* and not in response to the dictates of external necessity presented through the real constraints imposed by actual situations.

Thought, to the extent that it is rational, is also constrained by the limits imposed by logic as well as by certain empirical assumptions about the nature of reality--the assumptions that an ordered external world exists independent of perception, that such a world is governed by cause-and-effect relationships, and so on.

These real limits provide a sort of objective resistance in the process of organizing cognition. This resistance (which is a type of conflict), in turn, provides the sort of affective contrast within purely cognitive behavior which makes purely theoretical (non-applied) cognition incipiently pleasurable as well. Daydreams and fantasies, on the other hand, are less characteristically pleasurable than responses to events in the real world. This is true not only because they are tacitly recognized as internal responses to internal stimuli--as conscious responses to self-consciousness--that transpire within an internal reality but also because they are less constrained by the real limits imposed by objective necessity and logical thinking and are therefore less problematic and (as a consequence) less likely to elicit the kind of physical (motor-muscular) tensions which provide the possibility for the sort of tension-*reduction* that gives rise to positive emotional responses.

Sartre once remarked that the real world imposes limits on behavior (what he referred to as "a coefficient of adversity") that are subjectively experienced in a different manner than the interior (subjective) reality of images and symbols alone. In somewhat different terms, the individual tacitly recognizes whether he is responding to the real world (to actual situations), to *ideas* about the real world (concepts), or to ideas about an *unreal* world (fantasies). The real limits imposed by reality--whether direct or symbolic--create more significant conflict and therefore more significant conflict-resolution (pleasure) than that which is evoked purely by volition. In this sense, vicarious experience has a different motor-emotional tone--a different emotional resonance--than direct experience.

An individual implicitly knows that he is responding to images and symbols evoked from within and not from without, because the motor-emotional responses evoked by imagery and symbolism are substantially different than those elicited by responses to concrete situations.

3) Subjectivity reduces the intensity of commitment, because it generates ambivalence (and at least potential conflict) between the natural perceptions evoked by a situation and the purely imaginative perceptions

evoked by the same situation. In some conventional religions, for example, the individual is told that life is valuable and should be fully realized, but he is also told that there is life-after-death and that natural life is in many respects merely a preface to a potentially far more gratifying post-mortem existence in a purely spiritual realm. He is told that the psychological and social are inferior in any ontological hierarchy of values, to the spiritual, that the physical is properly subordinate to the metaphysical. Such a worldview blocks any passionate sense of social/political commitment within the natural world because it dilutes the significance of the natural/empirical world and reduces the sense of urgency associated with the limits (problems) imposed by an acceptance of one's own natural mortality.

11. Social Self-Actualization I

Man is naturally social. He requires others to survive and requires society, including culture, to provide the opportunities and artifacts required to be fully human in a rational-symbolic mode. This "social nature" is assimilated through the socialization-process, inductively, on the basis of cultural conditioning. Whether a person will be positively socialized and learn to ego-generalized, identifying with the well-being of others or of society-in-general <u>as a personal need</u>--whether he will become capable of some significant degree of "altruistic love"--depends on long and involved processes of learning that center primarily on child-rearing and the educational process during the earliest years.

Human beings are intrinsically active in a genetic sense. They are naturally <u>social</u> because of their extended dependency upon others during infancy and early childhood. Whether, and to what extent and in what form their social natures will manifest themselves is largely contingent on their subsequent cultural conditioning.

In a basic sense, and as already noted, man is naturally <u>moral</u> in the sense that a concern for the well-being of others and of society in general is logically implied by the unavoidable relationship between his inborn rational nature and his largely acquired (but logically implied) social nature. If man <u>requires</u> others and examines this "social imperative" rationally, he comes to the unavoidable conclusion that he is legitimately concerned with guaranteeing and advancing the best interests of others as a basis for his own effective self-actualization, Whether this moral sense is developed, on the other hand, and how it will be expressed is fundamentally contingent on whether, how, and to what extent the individual's rational and social natures have been cultivated in the first place. In this sense, personal morality is a tertiary development that is logically deduced on the basis of social values which are themselves inductive generalizations that depend on the way in which the individual's intrinsic cognitive capacities for assimilating and comprehending his own personal experiences have been cultivated (and particularly in the formative years of infancy and early childhood).

While individuals retain their unique differences, which are the unavoidable product of their own singular experiences in the world, their subjectivities (personalities) become increasingly "participational selves," part-functions of reality-in-general. Whether a person will demonstrate a "commitment to objectivity" to knowing and relating to the world-as-it-is (which can actually be looked upon as constituting a capacity for what might be termed "objective love," a sort of categorical concern for the larger and more encompassing aspects of the surrounding world, conceived in the broadest sort of terms, the sort of concern in which the individual's characteristic empathy for others as others his "altruism" is but one limited aspect of an overriding involvement in the larger world.

Self-actualizing people manifest a sort of "objective subjectivity," recognizing that man, in his highest expression, is necessarily a part-function of others, that self-actualization is virtually always contingent upon what might be termed "social self-actualization," as well as merely personal self-actualization.

In a basic sense, self-actualizing people are contingent upon other self-actualizing behavior. Self-actualizing behavior requires a supportive "humanistic" culture, It is quite possible, as philosopher Herbert Marcuse attests, to have a socially-promoted "false consciousness" which acts to subvert real human interests by teaching people to do things which are antithetical to their own real (that is, rationally and scientifically demonstrable) purposes. Such societies become entrapped in encompassing webs of self-delusion which, in turn, provide the justification for the kind of mystification and self-denial which contributes even further to an escalating sort of self-alienation. The members of such cultures are capable of becoming "dehumanized" or even becoming inhumane on the basis of moral principles which are not true moral principles at all.

Those who live under repressive social systems are ordinarily forced to sublimate, to flee to substitute satisfactions which subvert their real self-interests. In most instances, this is not a successful strategy for happiness, however, because the energy required for blocking, repressing and redirecting natural impulses is exorbitant and the return on the investment is typically far less than the satisfactions relinquished. The emotional "fix" works, but, as with any sort of fix, the addict builds up a tolerance to his own self-anesthetizing devices. A person who feels irrelevant and absurd within the existing social system may (as anthropologist Jules Henry so aptly points out) find temporary surcease from the "product therapy" of buying a new car or television set, but the next time he will need still more of a fix--a faster car or larger television set--for the same effect. Real self-actualization is intrinsically more satisfying than pseudo-self-actualization because it is a growth process in which experience dues not become deadened by infinite repetition.

In his book <u>New knowledge in Human Values</u> Maslow distinguishes between what he terms "high Nirvana"--the satisfaction to be attained through growth and self-transcendence--and "low Nirvana"--the state attained by a regression to childhood satisfactions. (Maslow 1971:125 or 425) The distinction is a good one, but in a sense it is also somewhat misleading, for, at basis, there are certainly two distinct types of "low Nirvana." It is necessary to distinguish between the <u>regressive</u> and infantizing effects of need deprivation and the <u>repressive</u> and dehumanizing effects of cultures which purposefully and systematically distort individuals' understandings of their own basic needs.

154

Self-actualization is largely a matter of transcending lower needs. It is also however, deeply involved with the identification of higher needs. "If I had been loved at seventeen," Flaubert once remarked, "what an artist I should be now!" (Camus--quoting Flaubert Correspondence --1965:14). Flaubert may have been right, but he could also have been wrong if he had lived in the wrong sort of society.

At basis, successful self-actualization is founded on five requirements:

1) the correct identification of human needs and/or potentialities;
2) the correct need-hierarchies, both psychological (developmental, subjective) and philosophical (objective);
3) the proper sequence and degree of need-gratifications in the course of personal psychological development;
4) an adequate degree and balance of basic need satisfactions with prevailing life-situations; and
5) a supportive humanistic social system which enables and encourages the highest development of human potentialities.

For all practical purposes, all of these conditions are dependent upon the existing social apparatus, belief systems, child-rearing patterns, educational practices and so on. In the final analysis, self-actualization is not "super-sanity" at all. It is, however, something that approximates a total sanity which requires extraordinary efforts to achieve within a society which is not committed to sane (humanistic and life-oriented) objectives. A society which is not committed to humanistic ends is not only less than sane. In a more significant sense, it postulates a type of insanity as a norm to be sought and subverts the possibility of real sanity altogether.

A significant question that arises naturally at this point relates to the relevance--and particularly the political relevance--of self-actualization in a non-self-actualizing society. Herbert Marcuse, among others, seems to be convinced that self-actualization is a potentially dangerous concept, even for well-meaning advocates of self-actualization as a social ideal, when they find themselves immersed in a repressive society. As Marcuse sees it, this is true not only because self-actualization provides an unrealistic goal which is not adaptable to such negative circumstances and which therefore interferes with the business of necessary political reform within the overall system, but also because it provides a sort of safety-valve for the fortunate few who are capable of availing themselves of such a utopian ideal, draining off their potentially subversive discontent into purely privatistic programs of self-perfection within a context of what actually constitutes an overwhelmingly inhumane frame of reference (providing a sort of anti-ideological retreat for the psychologically affluent within the midst of generalized emotional and cognitive poverty).

This latter point of view is probably in error for several reasons. To begin with, any significant sort of self-actualization would most probably imply the need for liberation from the dominant social delusions imbedded in the prevailing cultural ideology and would also probably generate an active commitment toward the creation of a much more humanistic and humanizing social system which would be at least potentially dangerous to the well-being of any truly repressive society. If nothing else, a self-actualizing person would "witness" to a way of life which implicitly negates and contradicts the status quo and which, in so doing, would probably augment a far greater degree of "revolutionary consciousness" among many segments of the general population than would otherwise be likely.

In addition, and far more significantly, this criticism of the viability of the self-actualization ideal makes the erroneous assumption that real self-actualization can be a purely subjective and personal goal. In point of fact--and as indicated earlier--self-actualization always functions as a moral commitment to a sane (self-actualizing) society and therefore implies rational activity in the direction of social reconstruction directed at a more enlightened culture.

This is not to deny that the self-actualizing person can be alienated. In a profound sense, all self-actualizing people in conventional (repression- and deprivation-oriented) societies are objectively alienated by definition.

156

Indeed, where self-actualization is accompanied by intellectual autonomy one is presented with the most radical sort of alienation possible when viewed from the perspective of conventional, conforming society. On the other hand, the alienation of the self-actualizing person is an intellectual alienation and stems from characterological objectivity and a highly flexible point of view. It is a decidedly different thing than the psychological and social alienation which are ordinarily used to describe diseases of adaptation within a particular culture.

In one sense, self-actualization is inherently revolutionary, because it implies a dedication to the most profoundly <u>human</u> values imaginable. On the other hand, the self actualizing person's commitment to the ideal of personal and social self-actualization does not blind him to the reality of the actual circumstances-at-hand. He works for change, however, realistically and not self-destructively. He is, in a sense, an <u>intellectual</u> <u>revolutionary</u> and not an <u>emotional</u> <u>rebel</u>. His disaffection is objective and rational, and he is perfectly capable of finding vast psychological (emotional) satisfaction within the struggle for a more humanistic world. Indeed, one of the ironies of self-actualization is that the self-actualizing person tends to <u>enjoy</u> his problems precisely because he is not <u>constrained</u> by them. He can approach them playfully, and his very "disinterest within commitment" makes him more reasonable and therefore more likely to solve the problems that exist than is the case of the individual who is more "personally" implicated, more ego-involved, in the course of action he is pursuing.

In short, the fact that he is a psychological "winner" actually helps him to aid the "losers," because one of the unfortunate aspects of chronically losing is that the losers also lose the frame of mind necessary to win. The self-actualizing social activist is sufficiently flexible to enjoy the game, because he is not fixated on either winning or warped into feckless anxiety by the consequences of continuously losing. Ironically, he can not only profit from the system while he works to change it, but if he were to cease doing so, his effectiveness would also diminish, because his capacity to win is largely based on the physical and psychological consequences of continued success in some sort of struggle to bring about significant changes in the world. In this respect, a topic which should be explored is that relating to self- sacrifice and self-actualization. To what extent is moral "witnessing" such as that exemplified by Albert Schweitzer possible or probable in self-actualizing people?

There are, on the one hand, those who hold that only a self-actualizing person has the inner strength and resources to be a martyr like Gandhi. They hold, in effect, that such intellectual commitment is only possible for those who have transcended normal concerns more or less altogether. On the other hand, there are those who maintain that any such disproportionate and almost monomaniacal (and fundamentally unplayful) dedication is ultimately a violation of self-symmetry and is fundamentally pathological, implying an abnormal emotional fixation at a lower-level of psychological functioning than true self- actualization requires. The problem remains to be fully explored.

Self-actualization theory is centrally involved in the question of values. It is an avowedly normative enterprise which rejects G. E. Moore's so-called "naturalistic fallacy" philosophy (which holds that it is impossible to derive values from facts, oughtness from isness). Self-actualization theory holds, on the contrary, that there are certain personal and social imperatives which are implicitly contained within a world of dynamically interrelated facts--that the prescriptive ultimately inheres within the descriptive.

The rationale for this approach might be represented as follows:

Philosophy
>	provides the intellectual rationale for the
>	metaphysical position of empirical naturalism and the
>	epistemological position of pragmatism
>	which provides the philosophical basis for

Science

    which offers a description of reality

    which tautologically confirms the empirical naturalistic/pragmatic world view

    leading to a new objective philosophy which is pragmatically (phenomenologically)

    vindicated rather than pragmatically verified

    which, among other things, yields a new scientific psychology

    which is phenomenologically verified as a basis for clinical psychology (therapy)

    which terminates in a new philosophical psychology

    which eventuates in self-actualization theory

    which provides the basis for a new normative science, including:

Social (Interpersonal) Ethics

Personal (Psychological) Ethics – involve concepts of personal pleasure, personal happiness, and such.

Scientific Ethics, an integrated and directive synthesis derived from the above combination.

Non-normative (descriptive) Science

Political philosophy (applied ethics)--the application of scientific ethics to the determination of social policies.

12. Social Self-Actualization II

At basis there are two kinds of societies. Those governed by the pleasure-principle, and those governed by the pain-principle. In essence, the pleasure-principle encompasses those societies which accept four fundamental notions: (1) the notion that pleasure (including the avoidance of non-pleasure and pain) is the highest personal (psychological) value; (2) the idea that happiness is the highest general (philosophical) value and that it constitutes the optimum realization of psychological pleasure over the maximum period of time commensurate with such a course of action; (3) the idea that self-actualization is the best operational means of realizing personal pleasure; and (4) that social self-actualization constitutes the highest interpersonal (ethical) value because it promotes the maximum realization of personal self-actualization of all through a social system that features a high degree of political liberty (by means of democracy) in combination with a high degree of economic equity (socially regulated economic activity) as a way of guaranteeing relatively equal opportunity for the self-actualization of all (which is ultimately a condition for the maximum self-actualization of each).

Societies organized around the "pain" principle are, on the contrary, societies which generally tend to accept the contrary notions: (1) that pleasure is not the highest personal (psychological) value; (2) that happiness is not rooted in the optimum realization of psychological pleasure; (3) that self-actualization is not the operational means of realizing happiness; and (4) that social self-actualization is neither the key ethical principle nor a necessary condition for personal self-actualization.

In general terms, societies organized on the pleasure-principle are humanistic in nature and generate a high degree of objective consciousness among their citizens. Those that are governed by the pain-principle tend to generate a high degree of subjective consciousness and to be non-humanistic (or even anti-humanistic) in their general orientation.

Freud while differing significantly in his concept of the pleasure-principle (eros) and pain-principle (thanatos), chose to be oriented to much this point of view, holding that the repression of natural sexual energies (eros) and the displacement of these energies into essentially non-sexual social activities lies at the very basis of all civilization. The Freudian worldview might be represented as follows:

Repressed eros leads to civilization, which gives rise to the anxieties of repressed living (the tensions of "self"-denial) which generate hate, aggression, and so on (i.e., thanatos), which are expressed in the guise of social disorders, which create the conditions necessary to justify increased repression and so on in a self-confirming cycle of negative (life-denying) and destructive behavior.

There are, in essence, three kinds of subjective non-humanistic societies: (1) those which are based upon objective scarcity in which there is no realistic expectancy for satisfying the deficiency within society in general; and (2) those based upon engineered (or coerced) scarcity within a society characterized by abundant possibilities for the satisfaction of deficiency needs; and (3) societies in which there is perceived scarcity despite conditions of objective abundance. Societies characterized by objective scarcity--as well as those in which scarcity is artificially created because an elite controls power and monopolizes wealth, thereby depriving the vast majority of need gratification--tend to generate what might be called "passive neurotic distortion" in the cognitive processes of its members.

A non-actualizing person who finds himself confronted with such real or forced deprivation-or, for that matter, any non-actualizing person--is confronted with a cycle of events which can be outlined as follows:

THE DEPRIVATION--SUBJECTIVITY--DEPRIVATION PROCESS

Deprivation creates "deficiency" motivation (fixation, inhibition and repression), which gives rise to subjectivity and loss of vitality (perceptual inefficiency, self-distortions, rigidity, ambivalence, ambiguity, et cetera), which give rise to poor problem-perceiving and problem-solving (cognition), which causes a low level of behavioral effectiveness, which gives rise to a low level of need satisfactions, and so on and on.

Subjective (non-humanistic) societies are all of those which are based on the pain principle and which in some significant degree center on the principles of self-denial and self-avoidance. Such societies promote and sustain a false sense of personal identity by means of collective self-delusion. In this way, they systematically frustrate the realization of human potentialities within society-at-large.

A subjective society is, in essence, any society which is not committed to humanistic principles related to the pleasure principle and which sustains conditions designed to frustrate the general realization of human potentialities.

Subjective societies differ primarily in the manner in which they manage oppression. Some oppression is a natural concomitant of objective scarcity. Some is a matter of social coercion, normally where an elite controls power and monopolizes wealth, systematically allowing the manipulation of behavior in the general population. Sometimes the oppression is effectuated by means of psychological manipulation in which the general population is co-opted into a false social ideology that emphasizes self-denial and scarcity in the face of objective abundance.

No purely <u>objective</u> society has ever existed. In all likelihood, no society which could legitimately call itself <u>objective</u> in any more than a rhetorical sense has ever existed even on an imperfect basis. This means that virtually all societies that have ever survived for any significant period of time have either been intentionally (volitionally) subjective- such as some contemporary Latin American "republics" or (until fairly recently) countries colonized by major powers or unintentionally subjective--the number of different cultures that may be construed to encompass such seemingly disparate entities as the "Peoples Republic" of China or the "demographic" republic of the United States.

What makes the subjective orientation so pernicious is that it is capable of using pleasure to subvert pleasure (i.e., self-actualization). As Smith and Debbins note: "The <u>potential</u> self is the norm, but the desires of the actual self are the contents for its realization" (Smith and Debbins 1948:78). By propagating a perverse concept of the potential self, subjective societies are capable of subverting the real nature of self- actualization and creating a new selfhood which is actually a type of self-alienation. In other words, by employing the profound principle that disease is no less organic than health, certain societies are fully capable of objectively presenting certain types of self- distortion as though they were positive aspects of selfhood and of using these as devices for exploitation rather than for true self-expression.

It is possible to have an <u>objectively</u> subjective society. In a pre-scientific and pre- industrial world, for example, poverty, scarcity and disease were facts for the average man and magic was a relatively "realistic" way of explaining the otherwise unaccountable. Indeed, the entire idea of the pleasure-principle as an object for human behavior was an exceedingly dubious proposition until relatively recently. Under such conditions, the institutionalization of self-denial--as through religion, traditional codes of sexual abstention, and such--were probably the most rational (and ultimately the most humane) way to minimize pain and maximize the small amount of pleasure available to the average man. As Freud was well aware, the superego can have a salubrious "libidinal" function if it is properly adjusted to the realities of the situation that prevails in the light of humane purposes.

In contrast to objective "scarcity societies" which generate subjectivity through passive neurotic distortion, there are societies characterized by relative affluence that create characteristically subjective cognitive processes by what may be termed "active neurotic distortion."

There are essentially two types of societies which create active neurotic distortion: (1) those that consciously engineer consent to policies that promote deprivation and scarcity among the population at large, and (2) those that unconsciously impose controls that promote deprivation and scarcity among the population at large.

Subjective societies that exist under conditions of objective affluence but which consciously impose controls that impose conditions of deprivation and a psychology of scarcity among the general population generally operate by means of what might be termed primary deprivation. They systematically dehumanize their peoples by keeping them fixated at a very low level of need satisfaction--pervasive hunger, chronic exhaustion, and so on. This acts as successful pacification. Social controls are direct, rudimentary and effective. Dehumanization creates stability and fosters fatalism. Everyone keeps busy just staying alive, and no one has the time nor inclination to entertain whimsical notions of pleasure and plenty (which are generally reserved for the elite). In its simplest expression, this might be viewed as a social conspiracy in which the many are systematically subjugated to the will of the few.

SOCIAL CONSPIRACY

Principle (ideology): Man is basically greedy and aggressive.

Policy: People must be controlled by an enlightened moral elite.

Practice: The systematic denial of popular autonomy (the radical restriction of civil rights, popular sovereignty, et cetera).

Consequences: Massive "dehumanization" with resulting existential anxiety based on the repression and inhibition of dynamic natural potentialities for self-determination, which gives rise on the social level to both conflict against the system (juvenile delinquency, and even conspiracies or--probably much more common- totalitarian regimes which seek to justify themselves after-the-affect on the basis of ideological justifications) and then tend to become institutionalized, absorbing the children of the original conspirators as somewhat muted victims of a System which is now conspiratorial only in an historical sense of the term). This is either unrewarded or actively punished, and compensatory cooperation with the system (which is rewarded by success and prosperity within the established frame of reference, both of which are used to justify the basic ideology of the system which then sustains and strengthens political policies and practices in a fundamentally self- confirming cycle.

THE EVOLUTION OF THE POWER ELITE FROM CONSPIRACY TO CO-OPTATION

A pleasure-ethic economic elite dominates and controls the pain-ethic masses in a traditional laissez-faire capitalistic system based on profit.

Profits require consumption by the masses of the goods and services produced by the economic elite.

High profits require high consumption which, in turn, requires mass wealth.

The masses therefore require wealth as a requirement for the success of the overall production-consumption cycle (that is, greater profits require greater production, which requires greater consumption, et cetera).

Wealthy masses are incipiently dangerous, because wealth is power, which poses an inherent threat against the established economic elite.

Therefore the economic elite must place greater and greater reliance on psychological controls--education, entertainment, communication, advertising, and so on (all of which are less expensive and ultimately more effective than external force and violence based upon police and armies).

But the growing sophistication and power of the masses (arising from growing wealth, leisure and education) makes overt wealth (conspicuous consumption) increasingly dangerous. There is, therefore, a tendency to downplay the difference between the "haves" and the "have nots." Such "leveling" serving as a sort of hedge and protective coloration against popular demands for radical economic reforms and the redistribution of wealth.

But altered behavior tends to alter belief. The children of the original conspiratorial elite begin to assimilate the democratic ethos which was originally a myth of domination and to regard it as a general social ideal.

The wealth of the entire culture begins to significantly transcend even the extreme wealth of particular individuals and groups. As a result, the quality of mass culture begins to rival and even go beyond that afforded by private means. For example, television, movies, schools, airlines, books, symphonies and so on, tend to become the collective possessions of all, regardless of differences in wealth and power. Cultural and consumption patterns become increasingly homogenized. In addition, the uses of wealth change as the growth of the economy accelerates. To remain constant, wealth must be continually re-invested, or "put to work." It cannot remain static. Phrased somewhat differently, consumption-wealth is not profitable. Increasingly, the emphasis falls on working capital, and less wealth becomes available for personal consumption or private expenditures.

As a result, the initial conspiratorial elite gradually becomes "domesticated." They find themselves castrated by their own pacification techniques--victims of their own democratic ideology and the rising standards of popular affluence which they increasingly share with the general public.

Eventually, the elite discover that their distinctive power lies primarily in production or control of wealth and not in its consumption (which is highly accessible to many who are not members of the small minority who are exorbitantly wealthy). In short, they become caught up within the System that they have created, and the difference between rich and poor, haves and have-nots, becomes less and less relevant in terms of consumption and much more a question of ownership and control. In this way, the economic system begins to function autonomously from its origins which envisioned profit as a means of providing for pleasure and consumption.

The end-result is an impersonal System in which production and power begin to govern people in a process which is progressively dehumanizing even for those who are ostensibly in control. In this way the conspiracy is co-opted by the technological-industrial system itself. The machine has assumed control from its masters.

Subjective societies which engineer consent to a pain-ethic despite conditions of objective affluence may also do so by imposing a false view of human nature.

This type of society functions by what might be termed relative deprivation and ordinarily operates in one or two basic ways. One way is to falsify the objective hierarchy of needs and to emphasize a lower type of motivation over higher types. A society which views man primarily in terms of his acquisitive needs for material goods, for example, while it may not actively deny higher goals for such things as intellectual and esthetic self-expression, may operationally deny their value by allocating rewards on a significantly different basis altogether. A population obsessed with material production and consumption is not physically denied access to non-material pursuits, but it is <u>psychologically</u> constrained to move in an entirely different (and therefore fundamentally non-self-actualizing) direction by the compelling nature of its contrary social conditioning.

In non-humanistic societies, a disproportionate emphasis is usually placed upon certain potentialities to the neglect of others, serving as an implicit falsification and denial of objective human possibilities. As a result, they disrupt the natural symmetry of the otherwise delicate system of social self-actualization and reduce the overall level of need-satisfaction among the general population.

In true self-actualization, Nemesis, the goddess of measure, must be heeded. As Lewis Mumford writes in his book <u>The Conduct of Life</u>: "Man loses his freedom through poverty, ignorance, and disease; and again, he may lose his freedom through the overdevelopment of a single organ or function, even through over-commitment to mechanical or social processes not under the control of the personality. This is why money and property, up to a certain point, are as much a condition for the development of the human personality as a direct access to the non-material elements of the culture, and to pretend that their absence does not matter is hypocrisy or dishonesty" (Mumford 1951:143).

In general, subjective cultures feature psychological rather than physical deprivation. Whatever the nature of the deprivation, the victims of social oppression are very similar to neurotics. The contrast, as Dollard and Miller have stated, is essentially that between "the contrast between the patient's current habits of repression and inhibition and the opportunities for gratification which exist in his environment" (Dollard and Miller 1965:318). "The neurotic starves in the midst of plenty; a beautiful woman cannot love; a capable man cannot fight; an intelligent student cannot pass his examinations. In every case the contrast is sharp between capacity to enjoy and opportunity to enjoy" (Dollard and Miller 1965:318).

It is possible to warp the objective hierarchy of needs without actually denying the reality of this hierarchy (and frequently while paying verbal obeisance to it) by tampering with the natural developmental hierarchy of needs. This can be done most effectively through child-rearing and education where, for example, a very young child may be forced to be "reasonable" in order to be loved. Thus, young children, who are seldom capable of sustaining reasonable behavior, are denied love as a way of encouraging rational development. The manifest, or purported, purpose of this treatment is to advance reason and therefore provide an effective basis for the fullest development of the child's self potential. The latent function is to block the development of real self-actualization by fixating the child at a deficiency-level of love-deprivation and, by so doing, to precipitate him into a self-confirming cycle of obsessive-compulsive behavior motivated by a prepotent need to be loved and respected. Such an approach is seldom intentional, but multiplied by millions of cases, such a pattern of child-rearing, although grotesquely oversimplified for purposes of illustration, can effectively terminate in a dominant type of socially-patterned character-defect.

On the other hand, subjective societies can also promulgate false concepts of human nature in a very direct manner. Again, to use a vastly oversimplified example, the society that teaches that sex is bad or that it should be denied or the society that maintains that man's highest destiny lies in the maximum production and consumption of material goods is (at least from the Maslowian point of view) misrepresenting the real nature of man. Such a society is propagating a destructive myth which not only leads away from the fullest expression of self-potential but which also provides a potential basis for rationalizing objectively <u>irrational</u> and <u>anti-humanistic</u> types of behavior. It should be stressed, of course, that most subjective societies feature a multiplicity of different approaches to self-distortion, different primarily in how these are combined and which are emphasized.

One of the ironic aspects of man's rational nature is that he can institutionalize his errors through education, child-rearing practices and such, and pass them on extra-genetically to generations as yet unborn as if they were true. The result is frequently a highly efficient system for producing what psychologist Erich Fromm has termed the "socially-patterned defective character." Such defects are not only elevated as virtues by society but are selectively rewarded to be subjectively satisfying. (Fromm 1956:42) "Socially-patterned defectives," notes Fromm, "don't have symptoms; they are symptoms."

Many non-humanistic cultures have become very adept at using short-term pleasure to subvert long-term pleasure, i.e. happiness attained through self-actualization. As Smith and Debbins note: "The potential self is the norm, but the desires of the actual self are the contents for its realization" (Smith and Debbins 11948:78). By propagating a perverse notion of the potential self, some societies have become adept at subverting the real nature of self-actualization and creating a new selfhood which is actually a type of self-alienation. A truly repressive society, for example, might be represented as follows:

REPRESSIVE SOCIETY

A society dedicated to non-humanistic ends and denying its people deep-seated personal satisfaction in the area of objective (real) needs

produces an "insane" people (a people motivated primarily by irrational response- tendencies)

who are characterized by a low degree of objectivity and vitality

which is reflected in a low-level of practical intelligence

which results in a low-level of behavioral effectiveness in terms of both the amount and quality of goods and services produced and the relevance of such goods and services to real (human) needs

which eventuates in a reduced capacity for fulfilling such real needs and so on and on in a negative synergistic process.

Phrased somewhat differently, this sort of society might also be represented as follows:

REPRESSIVE SOCIETY

A society organized on the pain principle (excessive work, self-denial, highly elevated levels of competition and war)

engenders sado-masochistic behavior (that is, self-denial and the prescription self-denial for others).

This results in pain (unhappiness, misery, frustration) and leads to a heightened drive-state, causing people to redouble their efforts on behalf of the dysfunctional socially sanctioned goals.

This causes immediate satisfaction, thereby reinforcing the pain principle and its associated social organization and also ultimately giving rise to an intensification of the overall misery which serves to guarantee a compulsive return to the pseudo-satisfactions derived from existing social values and so on and on in a negative self-confirming cycle.

When such a society gives rise to a high concentration of power (as in totalitarianism and certain types of oligarchy), it may generate what might be viewed as a dialectic of repression. This might be represented as follows:

THE DIALECTIC OF REPRESSION

Domination gives rise to real and incipient rebellion, which increases the need for domination, which enhances the likelihood of rebellion, et cetera, and so on.

Using the now familiar notion of the so-called Protestant ethic in conjunction with a relatively unfettered capitalistic political economy as one example of a repressive society, we might get the following:

CIRCULAR SOCIAL FRUSTRATION
(REPRESSIVE SOCIETY)

The Protestant ethic worldview (hard work, thrift, self-denial, the indefinite postponement of gratification and so on) working in conjunction with the materialistic consumption sub-ethic leads to various kinds of self-denying and self-distorting behavior, which are compounded by internal moral contradictions and inconsistencies (as between self-denial and consumption),

which generates anxiety (misery),

which expresses itself within the dominant ideology of the culture by seeking comfort in intensified efforts to reach precisely those goals (power and status by means of the competitive acquisition of goods),

which created the anxiety to begin with and which therefore serves to intensify the existing misery,

but which also lead to the consolidation and strengthening of the entire repression-system.

Repression has no necessary effect on intellectual potential (which IQ purports to measure) but it does have a significant effect on a persons practical ability to perceive and solve everyday problems (that is, <u>functional</u>, opposed to <u>potential</u> intelligence), and therefore frequently eventuates in a sort of <u>functional stupidity</u>.

REPRESSION AND FUNCTIONAL STUPIDITY

Repression generates anxiety (frustration),

which causes functional stupidity (perceptual rigidity, inappropriate response-sets, etc.),

which further augments anxiety (frustration),

which seeks alleviation through increased repression (reactive rigidity),

which leads to an aggravation of the total negative and self-destructive cycle of behavior.

PSYCHOLOGICAL REPRESSION AND FUNCTIONAL STUPIDITY

The heterosexual man who believes that sex is bad avoids women and therefore becomes obsessed with sex in the area of his deprivation-fixation,

which causes him to view much of contemporary theatre as a corrupting influence,

which stimulates him to seek to have certain performances banned and, generally, to attempt to control other peoples sexual behavior,

which makes him appear increasingly absurd in the eyes of many people, increasing the sum total of his anxiety and therefore leading to exaggerations of his original symptoms, to intensifications of his various moral postures, and so on and on, reinitiating and aggravating an intrinsically destructive behavioral process.

In his little read <u>Philosophical</u> <u>Fragments</u>, Karl Marx, who was one of the earliest advocates of psychological self-actualization theory, aimed his basic criticism of the relatively unbridled capitalism that existed during the earliest stages of the industrial revolution at the way in which it misrepresented the fundamental nature of man. In essence, his argument might be summarized as follows:

Capitalism's pathological concept of man regards value as residing primarily in things. The highest good lies in relationships to things. The ultimate value is to possess wealth; next is to use it, through consumption and through the exercise of power over others. Intellectual and esthetic behavior is secondary except where it contributes to the acquisition of wealth.

This blocks the basic human needs for love, intellectual development, beauty, etc, and breeds a sense of inarticulate frustration (existential anxiety) stemming from the blocking of these natural tendencies and needs.

This causes a compensatory reaction in the direction of those pleasure-mechanisms (that is, the acquisition and consumption of goods) which are socially encouraged. Even here, anxiety is created, however, because the value of consumption contradicts the value of production and acquisition, and it frequently elicits feelings of guilt in the consumer.

This leads to an exaggeration of the original sense of alienation (of being estranged from one's own nature as a man and as an individual) and creates still greater dependency on the existing system of alienation.

This culminates in a self-confirming, self-destructive cycle in which the individual seeks temporary pleasure within a context of overriding misery (the so-called "rat race"). Everything the individual does serves to strengthen his attachment to the dominant System and to confirm its practical effectiveness from the point of view of socially dominant values, but he also feels a gnawing and intensifying sense of discontent in his everyday living. He finds that he is unhappy "without reason." Ironically, the more miserable he becomes, however, the more he finds he must seek happiness in terms of the prevailing System which is, after all, the only solution available to his problem. He must have more status, more goods, and so on. To obtain these he must be more productive, and, ironically, his underlying disaffection with the System acts to the overall advantage of the System itself. At the same time, the externalized neurosis of the System (which is the central pathology of the individual as well) is strengthened by the very anxiety it provokes in its members. One does not question the System, not only because it is perceived as reality, or as "common sense," but also because the anxiety one already feels fosters a defensive rigidity, resulting in an even greater dependence on the System and leading to a compulsive retreat to its comfortable certainties as a way of dealing with an already overwhelming load of threatening doubt and anxiety. In many cases, the individual begins to wonder about his "sanity."

Outlined as a logical sequence of points, Man sees the dehumanizing forces of capitalism as undermining the ultimate value of self-actualization. His argument might be outlined as follows:

DEHUMANIZATION AND SELF-ACTUALIZATION

A technological economy activated by the competitive pursuit of wealth and power

requires profit derived from the sale of goods and services.

In general, maximum profit requires maximum production and maximum consumption.

In a growing economy, profit (wealth) must be reinvested in the economy in order to grow (that is, to appreciate in value relative to wealth in general); in other words, the most productive wealth is capital (wealth invested in further production).

Capital requires more production and therefore more consumption in order to grow (and reap more profits).

Since natural or biological needs are finite and satisfiable, capitalism requires the artificial manipulation of needs beyond the natural level (by means of advertising, propaganda and so on) in order to insure the sort of consumption-demands required to guarantee profitable production and the overall growth of the economy.

This results in a secondary or psychological type of "materialism" in which people are systematically addicted to gratuitous physical needs in order to guarantee increased production.

This leads to greater profit, enhanced production, improved production techniques (increased efficiency, automation, etc.), improved selling procedures, and so on.

This results in enhanced consumption which leads to a rise in expectancy with respect to future consumption-needs, which blocks psychological access to leisure (free-time), keeps individuals enslaved to the system, and generates additional increased consumption, therefore increasing production, advertising, expectancy, and so on and on in what is essentially a circular and self-confirming cycle.

With respect to contemporary American society, the neo-Marxist philosopher Herbert Marcuse envisions a process in which the development of productive forces leads to increased satisfaction of the material needs of growing numbers of people. It also, however, requires the creation of new needs as a way of insuring sufficient consumption and guaranteeing increased production and therefore increased profit. This profit could only grow effectively if it serves as capital, underwriting the artificial stimulation of more consumption needs, and so on and on.

Or--phrased somewhat differently--we have a situation in contemporary American society which Marcuse might diagram in the following manner:

CONTEMORARY AMERICAN SOCIETY (AFTER MARCUSE)

The Establishment (an economic elite of vested interests) directly and indirectly controls the reward-structure of our society thereby controlling the conditions of intellectual development that are based upon reward (reinforcement)--that is, information, communication, advertising, education, political parties, etc. In this way, it systematically brainwashes and economically implicates the general population.

This results in a sort of engineered consent in a pseudo-democracy in which the people are pacified by affluence and propaganda and therefore come to subscribe voluntarily, and even enthusiastically, to their own continued repression.

This lends additional power to the vested interests who gradually fall victim to their own pervasive environmental controls and become "brainwashed" by their own system.

This allows the system (the industrial-technological-economic apparatus) to function as a sort of impersonal "establishment" rather than as a conscious and intentional conspiracy.

All of this is exemplified in Marcuse's concept of "repressive consumption" which can be summarized as follows:

REPRESSIVE CONSUMPTION

The Power Elite (The Establishment) controls a system of advanced technological-industrial production which results in great wealth.

It uses this wealth to reward those who play the game effectively. The Establishment allocates money and products (thereby governing consumption) and creates demands for more goods by manipulating consciousness (by means of communication, education, advertising, and so on).

By manipulating rewards (reinforcements) they engineer learning and thereby increase consumption demands therefore increasing production, which increases and enhances greater consumption-addiction.

In his book entitled <u>Culture Against Man,</u> anthropologist Jules Henry, very much in the spirit of Marcuse, extends Marcuse's concept of repressive consumption by developing the related notion of what he calls "product therapy." His line of reasoning might be outlined roughly as follows:

CAPITALISM AND ALIENATION (AFTER JULES HENRY)

Materialistic alienation (the displacement of value onto money and things) gives rise to existential anxiety (a sense of not being fully alive to one's possibilities as a human being), which, ironically, is misdirected toward an exaggerated drive toward precisely those false values advanced by society expressed as a sort of product therapy, which serves to exaggerate the original symptoms and thereby leads to enhanced anxiety, which motivates more displaced activity in the guise of product therapy, which requires more money, therefore more work, and so on.

The point is not that real wealth does not increase under such conditions but--far more fundamental--that real <u>wealth</u> is not a sufficient condition for human happiness. Real wealth does increase under capitalism, although even here it increases disproportionately faster for the owners than for the workers. Automation reduces employment and makes production faster and more efficient. Other things being equal, the rate of production requires augmented marketing in order to increase the rate of consumption. Automation also increases profits over cost. It does not reduce demand, however, because demand is artificially stimulated by advertising, education, and so on. Salaries are increased. The people become wealthier. This reinforces growth and, in turn, insures the overall security of the System.

It does not increase free-time, however, because the increased salaries are needed for expanded consumption, and real free-time (leisure invested in self-cultivation which gives rise to self-knowledge) would be bad for the system, because self-determining individuals are extremely difficult to control and therefore pose a potential threat to society. Indeed, if people were free of the System--even in a purely psychological sense--for any significant period of time, they might attain a certain perspective on the System itself which would endanger the total mechanism of physical and psychological controls necessary for the continuance of the entire dehumanizing social order.

13. Social Self-Actualization III

～～～

Objective societies are societies based on the pleasure principle, advocating the fullest extent of self-expression and self-gratification for all individuals. The goal is a truly "sane society" in which we are reduced to outline form and, put in somewhat Freudian terminology, presented with the following:

THE SANE SOCIETY
SOCIAL SELF-ACTUALIZATI ON

A society organized on the pleasure principle

encourages erotic behavior (that is, "play"--behavior motivated by the pursuit of pleasure),

which gives rise to pleasure (and, in the long run, happiness),

which, in turn gives rise to learning and

which confirms the value of the pleasure principle as well as the social conditions associated with it,

and so on, in a self-confirming cycle.

Such societies are essentially humanistic and open to virtually any reasonable changes which are dictated by altered conditions or which are required by new knowledge. They also seek to guarantee whatever social conditions--rationality, science, material prosperity, health, leisure, and so on--which are required in order to encourage the highest degree of collective self-actualization. Such societies differ primarily in their ability to provide the conditions necessary for self-actualization.

At basis, the rationale behind the ideal of the objective society might be summarized as follows:

HUMANISTIC SOCIETY

Pleasure

Happiness

Science

Empirical naturalism (as a metaphysical principle) and
Pragmatism as an epistemological principle

Normative science--the application of scientific (objective) reason to normative questions relating to personal and social values

which yields a clear and verifiable theory of self-actualization as an operational ethic at the psychological level

which logically implies social self-actualization as an ethical orientation at the social level

which implies the necessity of political order combining a high degree of economic equity with an optimum expression of political liberty (representing democracy) which optimizes social self-actualization as well as personal self-actualization

which extends and perfects both science and the scientific worldview to reflect a progressively improved intelligence and increased knowledge

which serves to maximum happiness among the population in general and

which augments both the quantity and quality of personal pleasure by enhancing the level of need satisfactions thereby lessening deficiency-motivation and reinforcing the entire positive cycle of self-actualization.

In a sense, of course, this is just a special expression of the sort of synergistic process which has already been discussed at length: belief gives rise to behavior, which leads to experience, which emotionally confirms the behavior; which was itself at least a partial expression of the initial belief; and so on and so on.

Contrary to the notion that there is some sort of implicit conflict between technology and humanism, a truly humanistic (objective) society requires a high degree of technological development in order to reach fruition. This relationship can be summarized as follows:

TECHNOLOGY AND SELF-ACTUALIZATION

Technological industry

creates wealth

which augments consumption, satisfying psychological needs.

This allows man to transcend his preoccupation with physical requirements, altering values in a non-material direction and leading to a demand for the sort of social changes which are required in order to meet a whole set of new and essentially non-material needs (that is, greater leisure, more attention to aesthetic and intellectual concerns, etc.)

This leads to a heightened emphasis on creativity and intelligence

which acts indirectly to further perfect and rationalize the production-process

which eventuates in an economy of abundance

which precludes the necessity for traditional "work" altogether and

which allows for a virtually full-time preoccupation with "play" (self-expression).

The philosophy of self-actualization was, as indicated earlier, implicit in many of the earlier writings of Karl Marx. Marx held that personal value (happiness realized by means of self-actualization) ultimately required a humanistic society consisting of social self-actualization, the synergistic interrelationship with all social forces in a totally constructive and progressive system. This type of society, as he saw it, would ultimately contribute to a more or less total social unification (the Marxist "end of history" theory where all natural forces were synergistically unified in one positive and ongoing social process).

In essence, Marx's position held that self-actualization or constructive individualism requires personal freedom. Personal freedom, in turn, implies political deinstitutionalization (the minimizing of political restraints over personal behavior). Such deinstitutionalization can, however, only exist under conditions of social justice (public control over the production and distribution of goods). Such social justice necessitates a high degree of material prosperity (the availability of adequate wealth for all), as well as an enlightened moral philosophy (Marxism), which emerges naturally out of the dialectical process of progressive material evolution throughout history.

Fully conceived, self-actualization theory approximates the earlier self-actualization ideas of Marx, which might be diagrammed as follows:

THE MARXIST HIERARCHY OF PRESCRIBED VALUES FOR SELF-ACTUALIZATION

Explains, requires, and implements the following:

SCIENTIFIC PROCEDURES WITHIN A SCIENTIFIC WORLDVIEW

SOCIAL SELF-ACTUALIZATION

which necessitates and can only flourish on the basis of

TECHNOLOGY AND INDUSTRY

SOCIALISM

which implies the sort of economic affluence that it requires

Marx would have said "dialectical materialism" rather than "scientific procedures within a scientific worldview" but, since he tended to define dialectical materialism on the basis of a metaphysical position which corresponds to empirical naturalism and in terms of an epistemological position which approximates pragmatism (constituting a sort of sociological pragmatism), it seems justifiable to equate his Hegelian "materialism" with the sort of pragmatic naturalism that prevails in contemporary scientific philosophy.

In a sense, the sort of society which Marx--and by extension future self-actualization theorists like Maslow--envisioned would approximate the sort of "non-repressive" society envisioned much more recently by Marcuse:

NON-REPRESSIVE SOCIETY (MARCUSE)

Free reason (creative speculation)

subjected to science (scientific verification procedures)

gives rise to technology (applied science)

which leads to improved industry (automated technological production)

which requires a political system emphasizing social justice in the distribution of wealth among the general population

which generates popular affluence and

leads to mass leisure

which is a necessary condition for effective social-democracy

which sustains and advances free reason (civil rights, etc.) and so on in a self-confirming process.

The Marxist point of view on self-actualization also occurs substantially later, and in a significantly modified form, in the thought of the great American philosopher John Dewey. Dewey, with a much greater epistemological stress than Marx, holds that self- actualization is fundamentally contingent on effective problem-solving. This, he holds, is basically reliant upon experimental (scientific) thinking, which is only viable as a general mode of behavior in a social democracy. Accordingly, states Dewey, social democracy is capable of providing the basic political and economic conditions necessary for self- actualization in what is, again, a sort of positive synergism cycle. In a general sense, Dewey's point of view is well represented by his notion of the relationship between school and society which might be outlined as follows:

DEWEY ON THE RELATIONSHIP BETWEEN SCHOOL AND SOCIETY

THE GOOD OR SELF-ACTUALIZING LIFE

which logically requires all of the conditions it helps to sustain as a requirement for its own fullest development, in effect being based upon

SCIENTIFIC AND TECHNOLOGICAL DEVELOPMENT

which is merely a special expression of

TRAINED (EXPERIMENTAL) INTELLIGENCE

which, in turn, is based upon and requires

INDUSTRIAL DEMOCRACY ORGANIZED ALONG SOCIALISTIC (HUMANISTIC) LINES

ENLIGHTENED SYSTEM OF EDUCATION

The goal of the self-actualizing society is, at basis, sanity and all that this implies. In a sense, then, the "sane society" might be represented as follows:

THE SANE SOCIETY (SELF-ACTUALIZATION)

A society dedicated to humanistic ends

which envisions the satisfaction of objective (natural) human needs

produces a "sane" people characterized by emotional maturity and unhampered by covert irrational tendencies based on repression and inhibition.

Such a society is characterized by greater popular vitality and objectivity

which is reflected in improved popular intelligence

which results in enhanced behavioral effectiveness both in terms of the amount and the quality of goods produced and also in terms of the relevance of production and distribution with respect to enlightened (real) human needs,

which gives rise to an augmented capacity for fulfilling the objective human needs of the population-in-general and so on in a self-reinforcing, self-confirming process designed to satisfy basic <u>human</u> needs and, in so doing, to provide the conditions necessary for the maximum realization of <u>individual</u> needs as well.

Viewed still differently, the self-actualizing society might be outlined as follows:

THE SELF-ACUALIZING SOCIETY

Self-actualization (as a social goal) entails a high degree of education and self-expression

which requires leisure and the gratification of material needs,

which implies affluence (prosperity),

which necessitates industry,

which is based upon technology,

which is the application of science,

which is fundamentally a procedure for the objective verification of knowledge,

which, to be fully effective, requires radical new ideas

which are predicated upon the necessity of open enquiry,

which, in turn, requires an open society (a humanistic democracy which features intellectual and political freedom: freedom of speech, inquiry, association, press, and so forth),

which serves to augment popular self-actualization,

which increases "practical intelligence" (the ability to behave effectively) and therefore reasserts and strengthens all of the social conditions necessary for popular self-actualization (in what is fundamentally a self-confirming cycle).

The ideal society would probably be a society of self-actualizing scientists studying individual and social human behavior and using this knowledge to create a normative (prescriptive) science that would eventuate in a social ethic (a theory of social self- actualization) and a corresponding set of political principles and policies necessary to bring this ethical system into practical reality. Barring this, it would, in all likelihood, be a society organized along the principles determined by such a scientific/intellectual elite--something akin to the Planners who would have supervised changes in Skinner's famous utopian community of Walden II in the contentious novel of the same name but administered in a purely technocratic way by experts in the various areas vital to social life (corresponding roughly to the so-called Managers in Skinner's vision of the perfect world).

Contrary to virtually all self-actualization theorists, Skinner was not a democrat. He felt that there was a science of human behavior (in his case, behavioristic psychology) which could properly determine not only human needs but the optimum expression of such needs and the optimum relationship between them, in the life of society. He held that truth was objective and scientifically determinable and not a matter of uninformed popular opinion that could be determined by popular vote

In a sense, of course, no truly humanistic society of this sort has ever existed. Virtually all recorded societies have either been explicitly subjective--such as many contemporary Latin American "republics" and various of the existing Arab Emirates and kingdoms--or implicitly subjective--which might be viewed as a spectrum of possibilities encompassing everything from the "People's Republic", of China to the present "democratic" government of the United States.

With respect to self-actualization, there are two basic types of objective societies: those based on objective conditions of scarcity and those based upon objective abundance but nevertheless governed by ideologies featuring scarcity as a central and controlling concept.

Scarcity Societies: Human societies based on objective conditions of scarcity are forced to manage pain in order to maximize pleasure. This can be done in two ways: (1) by reducing the general standard of living in such a way as to provide all with a basic. minimum of need-gratification or (2) by restricting the ideal of self-actualization to a selected elite, using the bulk of the population as a deprived "service-class" in order to maximize the humanistic possibilities for a chosen few.

In general, the first course of action is exemplified in such liberal social-democracies as contemporary Denmark and Sweden. The second course of action is, of course, the idea inherent in so-called "Athenian democracy," that is, the idea of a dual morality in which the pleasure principle (self-actualization) is applied to the dominant elite while the pain principle (based on self-denial) is applied to the subordinate "service" classes.

It is quite possible to be self-actualizing as an individual in a society such as ancient Athens where a "sell-actualizing" subculture subscribes to a "master morality" of pleasure and, at the same time, systematically subjugates a "slave" population doomed to survival within scarcity. Whether such a subculture can be justifiably characterized as "self-actualizing" is, of course, argumentative, but certainly some instances of individual self- actualization can and did occur under these conditions.

Abundance Societies: Humanistic societies based on abundance--and many would argue that the United States and most of Western Europe today is sufficiently affluent to become such societies given certain significant modifications in social policy--have attained such an advanced level of scientific, technological, and industrial development that they have managed to transcend the necessity of traditional scarcity, as well as the large expenditures of manual labor typically associated with such scarcity, more or less altogether. Employing the effective application of advanced mechanization procedures and the maximum utilization of computerized and automated controls over production, such a society has managed to make affluence, and therefore the leisure necessary for self-actualization, possible as a viable popular ideal. Work, in the sense of coerced physical and psychological activity, is tending to disappear under such conditions and is increasingly being replaced by volitional growth-oriented activities (that is, "play"). Production--transposed into an organizational and intellectual challenge rather than merely dull toil--becomes essentially an avenue of autonomous self-expression, a sort of esthetic process rather than a matter of mere drudgery.

In the United States today, it is frequently contended that ostensibly humanistic ideals have been reconstrued to promote what is merely an ostensibly humanistic system that might be better viewed as a sort of "capitalistic technocracy." Such a system is frequently represented as follows:

CAPITALISTIC TECHNOCRACY

"Self-actualization" (defined as the right to be "happy" as a consumer) requires leisure and the gratification of material needs,

which implies affluence (prosperity),

which is based upon industry,

which is an expression of technology,

which is an application of science defined in substantially non-humanistic terms to encompass the physical and biological sciences but to exclude the social sciences and the humanities,

which is used for the objective verification of knowledge in relevant "scientific" (physical or material) areas,

which allows for intellectual and political freedom in non-controversial (non-humanistic) areas--that is, for the full civil rights <u>within</u> the established social-value system,

which augments popular "self-actualization" within the accepted non-humanistic frame-of-reference, thereby militating against the likelihood of political dissent and

which increases "functional intelligence" (that is, the ability to behave effectively within the established frame-of-reference) and which reinstitutes and reasserts the entire cycle in a fundamentally self-confirming manner that actually sustains and promotes non-humanistic goals of belief and behavior.

The outcome of this process is perhaps apparent. There is a high degree of freedom. Virtually everyone can do what he wants. On the other hand, what the average person <u>wants</u> is rigidly programmed by the nature and availability of the options which are made available and which are defined as desirable. Everything changes in an overriding context of constant (and frequently invisible) assumptions. Certain assumptions are not questioned and, indeed, are exempt from criticism by political edict. In the former Soviet Union, for example, history, while ostensibly "scientific," was actually ideological. It served a political function in a culture which, for all practical purposes, kept its political values beyond the ken of critical scrutiny. One was perfectly free to make the most radical conjectures about such topics as astronomy, archaeology or particle physics (and, indeed, was often encouraged to sublimate by doing so), but the social sciences, the humanities, and the arts were carefully controlled and made to conform to the official point of view.

This does not always work smoothly, of course. In the famous Lysenko controversy after World War II, for example, Stalin made the error of extending ideological concerns to an area of agricultural genetics (which also had political implications), and offered official support to a neo-Lamarckian theory of wheat cultivation which simply made no scientific sense (or, at least, very little). In doing so, he violated the established "technical morality" of Soviet culture and injected political considerations into the "pure science" base of his own technological-industrial complex. As a result, he caused severe difficulties in the area of agricultural production which had very negative economic consequences on a purely practical level.

In a far less drastic sense, in our own country, we are all purportedly free to exercise a variety of civil rights--freedom to speak, freedom of press, freedom to associate, and such--within very broad limits. In practice, however, these rights are severely limited. I am very free to read whatever newspaper I choose, but very few people are free to publish newspapers. I am quite free to speak and associate with whom I choose, but if I do so, I may very well endanger my well-being by jeopardizing my future employability in selected areas or even my right to travel to certain countries outside our borders.

14. Typology II - Types and Levels of Self-Actualization

A central problem in self-actualization theory pertains to whether and to what extent a person can be properly characterized as self "actualizing" without being totally--that is, both affectively and cognitively--involved in a total pattern of self-actualizing behavior. Perhaps a simpler way to view this question is to ask whether a person can be *personally* (psychologically) self-actualizing without also being committed to the *social self-actualization* of others and therefore "moral" in a more encompassing and interpersonal sense than that associated with merely being "happy" in a narrow psychological way.

This is a difficult problem to address, but, in a general sense, the answer appears to be a qualified "yes." It *is* possible to be psychologically "good-for-one's-self," experiencing a high degree of ongoing pleasure and pursuing personal happiness, without at the same time being committed to any particular course of moral action with respect to others.

This would appear to happen in three basic situations. It would appear likely to occur as a *phase* of personal development--a sort of proto-self-actual--the case of individuals who are evolving towards fully-functioning self-actualization but who have not yet graduated to a degree of knowledgeability sufficient to establish a full sense of reasoned morality with respect to others.

In this sense, a potentially self-actualizing person normally progresses through four basic stages of affective/cognitive development:

1) The earliest hedonic phase in which his conative behavior is shaped into volition through autonomic (motor-emotional) conditioning during the earliest weeks, months and years of life;

2) The gradual cognitive organization of effective hedonic behavior as an overriding commitment to some particular mode of realizing personal happiness as a sustaining pattern of conduct;

3) The gradual realization that interpersonal happiness logically implies the happiness of others--social morality--as an unavoidable corollary of personal happiness; and

4) The cognitive/affective integration of pleasure, personal happiness, and interpersonal morality as a total and encompassing ethic--in which there is a continuous, self-perpetuating and self-reinforcing interaction, terminating in a positive synergism cycle between the experience of pleasure at the psychological level, the organization of pleasures on a cognitive/affective level (personal happiness), the rational extension of happiness to encompass the well-being of others, and the overall ethical Gestalt that is manifest in a fully functioning process of generalized self-actualization (which might be actually viewed as a sort of "self-Self-actualization") in the sense that the needs of the psychological self are reconciled with the intrinsic needs of a teleologically-emerging ontological reality).

It is clearly possible--although not necessarily inevitable, since much depends on moral training in the essentially pre-rational eras of infancy and early childhood--that an incipiently self-actualizing person will go through a phase in which he is essentially happy in a *personal* sense without yet comprehending the full *interpersonal* implications of his own commitment to self-actualization, narrowly and subjectively conceived.

In still a second scenario--and Maslow does not comment significantly on this-- there would appear to be two essentially different types of self-actualization: (1) that which ideally terminates in a fully functioning, generalized self-actualization, and (2) that which reaches its highest expression in an essentially partial (and more or less compartmentalized) arena of human activity. In other words, "molar" self-actualization of the more encompassing sort is based on broad philosophical concerns and involvements. It is characterized by a pervasive intellectual curiosity directed toward the kind of categorical humanistic questions such as, Who am I? Where am I going? What can I hope for?

The "molecular" self-actualization of the more specialized sort-- say that of the composer or of the mathematician as opposed to that of the novelist, the psychotherapist, or the philosopher--is essentially compartmentalized in an arena of involvement that does not necessarily relate to the overall concern of others in any direct way and that may remain essentially undeveloped in the social realm of interpersonal relationships. Such an individual is objective and happy but within a radically restricted area of activity that may not be conducive to the development of a fully conceived moral view of the world. In such instances--individuals like the composer Richard Wagner and the nuclear physicist Niels Bohr might serve as examples--it is possible for a person to be essentially self-actualizing at both a cognitive and affective level (with a positive synergy operating at and within this level) without at the same time developing his moral and ethical nature to any appreciable degree. This very insularity provides him with the opportunity to be either amoral or immoral without suffering many of the affective consequences that would normally assail the self-actualizing generalist who is exposed to a broader range of possibilities.

Finally, there appears to be a third scenario in which the person undergoes the sort of socialization that produces a sort of pathological *pseudo-self-actualization* that actually focuses upon patterns of behavior that would be assessed as negative and immoral from the point of view of the fully functioning, self-actualizing person. Such an individual--and

Hitler or Stalin are perhaps good examples here--is vehemently subjective and is sufficiently intelligent and impassioned to create a highly neurotic surrogate-reality replete with a warped commitment to an objectively immoral agenda for social action. This substitute subjective-reality-- which is probably in most cases the product of systematic deprivation and distortion in the developmental years--is projected as a program for passionate intellectual action.

Such a person, paradoxically, experiences the world very intensely. He optimizes pleasure, and he experiences personal happiness within a virtually "closed" subjective worldview--a worldview that is fully capable of producing a sort of positive synergism as long as it expresses itself in a totalistic social system that accepts it as a legitimate view of reality. Such subjectivity requires either isolation or extraordinary political power over others in order to become a perverse and negative correlate of real self-actualization. In the case of Hitler, it was probably his years of comparative isolation both as a social "outsider" and in prison that allowed him to rationalize and externalize his delusions, and the explication of his beliefs in his magnum opus, <u>Mein Kampf</u> was probably a profoundly pleasurable experience. On the other hand, it was the political process that he created and subsequently succeeded in establishing in National Socialist Germany that provided him with the sort of *social* reinforcement that allowed him to use his Nazi program as a self-reinforcing system of affective/cognitive-fulfillment.

Phrased somewhat differently, it was Hitler's ability to convince others that his *subjectivity* was *objective*--in conjunction with his capacity to *objectify* his *subjectivity* through political power--that made him capable of generating social (and therefore objective) confirmation for his own beliefs and actions. Whether one likes it or not, Hitler was probably a very "happy" man from the time that he was released from prison after his abortive putsch in Munich until the time that he committed suicide in the Berlin bunker.

In a sense, he predicted his own end as one possible scenario in his writings, and his very death was a partial confirmation of his vision. Certainly his death does not disqualify his actions, because life is inherently tragic, and everyone's life--self-actualizing or otherwise--ends in death. This is one of the reasons that censors frequently make a grave error in assuming that virtually any kind of immorality can be sanctioned so long as the villain is killed in the end. *Everyone* is killed in the end, and even children recognize that an exciting life that leads to death with a bang is probably a better choice than an innocuous existence that leads to death as a whimper.

If Hitler had remained a third-rate landscape painter in Vienna, he would probably not have become the epitome of evil. Conversely, however, he would probably not have been as fully alive and therefore "happy" in the *psychological* sense as he probably was. If Stalin had become the Russian Orthodox priest that he was initially training to be, millions of people would not have died, but Stalin as *Stalin* would not have realized the sort of evil sense of psychological consummation on a purely subjective level that he may very well have finally attained.

If Hitler and Stalin can be viewed as examples of malign (immoral) pseudo-self- actualization, there is also the possibility of what might be termed benign (moral) pseudo- self-actualization. In such a case, the individual is committed to a subjective point of view (frequently metaphysical or theological in nature) which encompasses a positive moral involvement that is intended to benefit others. As in the case of malign pseudo-self actualization, such cases also involve a totalistic community of true believers within which the person operates.

Thus, to provide an extremely controversial example, Mother Teresa of Calcutta is generally recognized as an exceedingly moral person. She is also, in her own way, probably a very happy person. Viewing her activities from outside the Christian (and particularly the Roman Catholic) point of view, however, she operates in a manner analogous to that of a Hitler or a Stalin.

She subscribes to a point of view (Roman Catholicism) that is intensely subjective from an empirical-naturalistic frame of reference, encompassing heaven and hell, angels, miracles, and so on.

She operates essentially within a community of true believers (the other members of her religious order and the more general community of her faith) who subscribe to essentially the same subjective point of view.

She perceives the world accurately within the context of this overriding set of subjective (and therefore inaccurate) beliefs.

She is therefore behaviorally effective in ministering to the needs of others as directed by the overriding ideological commitment of her religion.

Her belief-system is therefore reinforced both within her own community of believers and within other communities, both theological and humanistic, which share her general concern for the well-being of others. This allows her to operate within the confines of a positive synergism cycle.

A subjective reality-orientation combined with the high-high configuration which is clearly possible--presents an interesting picture. Such a person subjectively misconstrues both the world and himself. He passionately pursues a false and dysfunctional program of personal commitment, and he processes fallacious information quickly and effectively in pursuit of his misconceived ends. Such a person can only be viewed as bright, passionate and--from the point of view of social morality--very dangerous. Such an orientation has the advantage of producing the maximum "psychological high" (pleasure) on a continuing and self-perpetuating basis while, at the same time, generating the social conditions that have a potentially disastrous effect on popular objectivity, general sanity, and the sort of social order that is capable of creating and sustaining such objectivity and sanity. It could well be argued that such a person would--in the long run or on balance--create the kind of "insane society" that would work against the real best interests of everyone including himself. Maslow was fond of reversing the old saying that "Time heals all wounds," by stating that "Time wounds all heels."

Unfortunately, life is short, and passionate neurotics do not ordinarily live long enough to undergo the long-range consequences of their own self-delusions. They frequently experience immense psychological gratification from exploiting their own pathologies. In a similar sense, the notion that the passionate neurotic does not prosper *on balance*--that the total picture during his own lifetime is negatively weighted toward frustration and pain rather than toward gratification and pleasure--does not parse out. Kant was sufficiently disturbed by the patently unjust rewards provided to "evil" men that he used this as one rationale for establishing the existence of a personal God who would, among other things, punish such individuals in the hereafter. For the naturalist, this is not a satisfactory answer, and, if there is an answer, it seems to reside primarily in the province of psychotherapy and criminal justice rather than in the inexorable workings of a world viewed as intrinsically programmed to correct injustice by virtue of its own natural consequences over time.

Hitler and Stalin were such passionate neurotics. The first died, still in command, after an impressive career that almost brought the world to the edge of apocalypse. The other died at an advanced age (also still in power) from what were probably natural causes.

In view of these considerations, it is clear that self-actualization is not a simple phenomenon. It actually exists on a continuum.

PASSIVE NEUROTIC DISTORTION
(Deprivation and Dissensus)

Predetermined nature of man

Giving rise to predetermined behavior (deficiency- motivation)

Blocking of deficiency-need gratification

Leads to fixation at level of blocked needs

Creating preoccupation with blocked needs--interference with normal sequence of psychological development--unconscious displacement of need-gratification through compensatory activities

Which gives rise to distorted ego-processes (deficiency motivation)

Which interact with the predetermined nature of the world.

15. Objective Love/Peak Experiences

Moments of emotional transport, or ecstasy, may, of course, grow out of either Apollonian or Dionysian experience. The basic difference would seem to reside in the fact that ecstasy is for the Apollonian essentially an abnormal, or supernatural, affair growing out of an aggravation of tensions within normal experience. From the Dionysian point of view, however, it is expressed as a full realization of the normal--that is, as a natural "bringing to fruition" of the extraordinary qualities which are implicit within the commonplace. As Sorokin states:

"Eliot's 'moments in the rose-garden,' 'the moment in the draughty church at smokefall,' 'lost in a shaft of sunlight,' in the 'whisper of running streams and winter lightening,' or the moments when 'music [is] heard so deeply that it is not heard at all, but you are the music while the music lasts,' or the moments 'I can only say, there we have been: but I cannot say where . . . beyond any meaning we assign to happiness'--these and similar supraconscious moments occur in the life of almost all individuals. They are the highest peaks of creativity reached by an individual in his whole life" (Sorokin 113).

Maslow's peak experiences, on the other hand, are essentially Dionysian in nature, expressing themselves as direct "subjective" unions with the non-self, a sense of immediate participation in or identity with some aspect of the external world. As Brown states:

"The Dionysian is no longer an artist, he has become a work of art [68]...

Hence <u>he does not negate any more</u>. This, says Nietzsche, is the essence of the Dionysian faith [70].... Dionysus is the image of the instinctual reality which psychoanalysis finds on the other side of the veil..."(Brown 174-175).

Regardless of how the mystical unity with the non-self is defined, it does not seem justified to say that <u>differences</u> actually disappear in the state of mystical transport. In general, it is not the differences as such but, rather, the perceived significance, or relevance, of these differences which is altered. In most cases, there is a sense of direct participation in the experimental process itself which is variously described as either a total sense of <u>being</u> (i.e., being available to experience or of being totally sentient) or <u>non-being</u> (i.e., being so immersed in experience as to lose oneself as an experienced object and, hence, of no longer being differentiated at all). This is, in turn, accompanied by a sense of the total irrelevance of traditional cognitive or analytical distinctions. This may even express itself as an active aversion to the usual cognitive fragmentations or objectifications of the experiential continuum. The traditional categories and classifications are totally eclipsed by the total prepotency of the instant itself, and one becomes, in Martha Graham's words, "present to the instant."

"I am against knowledge," states Henry Miller. "I abhor it. I loathe it. I want to become more and more ignorant, more quiet, more vegetative, more ruminative, more omnivorous, carnivorous, herbivorous. I want to stand still and dance inside" (Miller 1963).

Or, as Will James describes his own mystical reactions under the influence of nitrous-oxide gas, all intellectual resistance "... vanishes in a higher unity in which it is based; ... all contradictions, so-called, are but differences; ... all differences are of degree ... all degrees are of a common kind ... unbroken continuity is of the essence of being; and ... we are literally in the midst of <u>an</u> <u>infinite</u> to perceive the existence of which is the utmost we can attain" (James 1956:295).

To end such an experience is to feel oneself once more "earthbound." "... as sobriety returns, the feeling of insight fades, and one is left staring vacantly at a few disjointed words and phrases, as one stares at a cadaverous-looking snow-peak from which the sunset glow has just fled, or at the black cinder left by an extinguished brand" (James 1956:294).

It is frequently held that the mystical experience is "a mark of inadequate art."

That might account, as philosopher Susan Langer suggests, "... for the fact that all very great artistic conceptions leave something of mysticism with the beholder; and mysticism as a metaphysic would then be the despair of implicit knowledge, as skepticism is the despair of discursive reason" (Langer 1957:224).

The truth, however, may lie in the opposite direction. It may be that "art" is only required by those who find reality itself esthetically (intrinsically) unrewarding. For the true Dionysian, life <u>is</u> art--a continuous and self-sustaining process of esthetic activity. As philosopher Norman O. Brown states: "The <u>animal symbolicum</u> (Cassirer's definition of man) is <u>animal sublimans</u> committed to substitute symbolical gratification of instincts for real gratification, the <u>desexualized</u> animal. By the same token the <u>animal symbolicum</u> is the animal which has lost its world and life, and which preserves in its symbol systems a map of the lost reality, guiding the search to recover it" (Brown 167).

In the final analysis, then, <u>if</u> the perennial philosophy which lies at the core of the Eastern wisdom is to be regarded as a type of mysticism, it is important to recognize the fact that it is clearly a type of mysticism which deviates markedly from the dominant Apollonian approach which characterizes the Western mystical tradition in three basic respects.

First, it is, in a peculiar sense, a practical, or pragmatic, sort of mysticism. The goal of Zen is neither insight nor ecstasy in the most common sense of those terms but, rather, a full realization of everyday, commonplace experience. For Zen, the ultimate goal of life is not truth but value, and value is always at basis nothing more than life itself, fully realized through a type of objective awareness--consciousness without self-consciousness--which is necessarily non-cognitive in nature.

Second, of course, Zen is not an indirect, symbolic release of tensions in the usual Apollonian sense. At basis, the Zen insight is that there is no Zen insight--that truth is at basis no insight at all but a total non-verbal and essentially ineffable "awakening" to the fact that the only real "truth" is that truth which lies only in its own negation and in the simple affirmation of the purely subjective experiential process itself, "the aimless, self-sufficient life of the 'eternal now'" (Watts 1957:151).

Finally, while the way of Zen may be communicated verbally, it is never really conveyed this way. The ultimate test of Zen can never be cognitive but only existential,

"... Zen avoids the entanglements of religiosity and goes straight to the heart" (Watts 1957:150). In this way, the "entire framework of abstractions is shattered to fragments" (Watts 1957:150). As Zen master Daisetz Suzuki states, the unconscious is "... the most intimate thing to us and it is just because of this intimacy that it is difficult to take hold of, in the same way as the eye cannot see itself. To become, therefore, conscious of the unconscious requires a special training on the part of consciousness" (Suzuki 1956:131).

This special training does not lend itself to the traditional approaches of verbal didacticism. It is communicated primarily through action language and through object language and not through the medium of words. This can be observed, among other ways, in the special attention which Zen traditionally affords to the physical body itself and to its functions.

As Watts indicates, for example: "Whether Zen is practiced through Za-Zen or Cha-no-vu or Kendo great importance is attached to the way of breathing... - the relationship between breathing and 'insight' is not yet altogether clear. But if we look at man as process rather than entity, rhythm rather than structure, it is obvious that breathing is something which he does--and thus is--constantly. Therefore grasping air with the lungs goes hand-in-hand with grasping at life" (Watts 1957:190-191).

16. PEAK EXPERIENCES

In a very basic sense, the motive behind all behavior is the realization, the bringing to closure, of ongoing behavior. The morphogenesis of knowledge is, then, ultimately determined by the morphology of behavior and not by the structure of the universe viewed as something apart. "Overt intelligent performances," Gilbert Ryle once stated, "are not clues to the workings of minds; they are those workings."[1]

Behavior is both purposive and organized. The end of all behavior is the anticipated motor-affective realization of certain acts. Accordingly, each act is merely a step in a sequence of activities that is, in turn, both consummatory to that which precedes it and heuristic to that which follows. [2] The success of the entire venture is sustained by the tension of felt-need. It is directed by the logic of action. It is verified by the sort of motor-affective "feel" of ongoing experience that may ultimately resolve into a sense of total ideo-motor-affective "closure" with respect to the problem at hand.

All intuitive behavior is essentially conative, consisting of the willed realization of uncompleted acts. Since all action consists of organized energy, in a continuous process of reorganizing itself, the implicit goal of every act is the completion, or realization, of its own inherent form. In a sense, then, cognition follows the natural organization of spontaneous behavior and, as Suzuki comments with respect to Zen,

"The truth is that what involves the totality of human existence is not a matter of intellection but of the will in its most primary sense of the word. The intellect may raise all kinds of questions--and it is perfectly right for it to do so--but to expect any final answer from the intellect is asking too much of it, for this is not in the nature of intellection. . . . The intellect . . . is something floating on the surface of consciousness. It is not the ultimate reality itself. The intellect is needed to determine, however vaguely, where reality is. And the reality is grasped only when the intellect quits its claim on it.[3]

The full realization of any significant sequence of ongoing behavior--whether overt and physical or covert and symbolic--is experienced as a sense of affective consummation which is essentially <u>esthetic</u> in nature. Such a sense of consummation occurs in those instances where behavior is both congruent with intent and, at the same time, adapted to the requirements of the situation itself. The resulting sense of total fulfillment may on certain occasions border upon the ecstatic and has been variably described by a number of different observers. In his essay "Return to Tipasa," for example, novelist-philosopher Albert Camus makes the following comments on his feelings while visiting the ancient Roman ruins at Chenoua on the Bay of Tipasa near Algiers:

"...I finally got through the barbed wire and found myself among the ruins. And under the glorious December light, as happens but once or twice in lives which ever after can consider themselves favored to the full, I found exactly what I had come seeking, what, despite the era and the world, was offered me, truly to me alone, in that forsaken nature. From the forum strewn with olives could be seen the village down below. No sound came from it; wisps of smoke rose in the limpid air. The sea likewise was silent as if smothered under the unbroken shower of dazzling, cold light From the Chenoua a distant cock's crow alone celebrated the days fragile glory. In the direction of the ruins, as far as the eye could see, there was nothing but pock-marked stones and wormwood trees in perfect columns in the transparence of the crystalline air. It seemed as if the morning were stabilized, the sun stopped for an incalculable moment in this light and this silence, years of wrath and night melted slowly away. I listened to an almost forgotten sound within myself as if my heart, long stopped, were calmly beginning to beat again. And awake now, I recognized one by one the imperceptible sounds of which the silence was made up: the figured bass of the birds, the sea's faint, brief sighs at the foot of the rocks, the vibration of the trees, the blind singing of the columns, the wrestling of the wormwood plants, the furtive lizards I heard that; I also listened to the happy torrents rising within me. It seemed to me that I had at last come to harbor, for a moment at least, and that henceforth that moment would be endless. But soon after, the sea rose visibly a degree in the sky. The magpie preluded briefly, and at once, from all directions, birds' songs burst out with energy, jubilation, joyful discordance, and infinite rapture. The day started up again. It was to carry me to evening."[4]

In his final reminiscences, philosopher and art historian Bernard Berenson looks back on his own fleeting moments of self-fulfillment.

"As I look back on fully seventy years of awareness and recall the moments of greatest happiness, they were, for the most part moments when I lost myself all but completely in some instant of perfect harmony. In consciousness this was due not to me but to the not-me, of which I was scarcely more than the subject in the grammatical sense. In childhood and boyhood this ecstasy overtook me when I was happy out of doors. Was I five or six? Certainly not seven. It was a morning in the early summer. The silver haze shimmered and trembled over the lime trees. The air was laden with their fragrance. The temperature was like a caress. I remember--I need not recall--that I climbed up a tree stump and felt suddenly immersed in itness. I did not call it by that name. I had no need for words. It and I were one."[5]

In a sense, of course, such moments of pure motor-affective realization come very close to Bergson's idea of truly liberated intuition. They are also strikingly similar to Zen satori and bear a remarkable kinship to the Freudian concept of pure unrepressed sexuality. "The idea" as Watts comments with respect to Zen enlightenment, "is not to reduce the human mind to a moronic vacuity, but to bring into play its innate and spontaneous intelligence by using it without Forcing it."[7]

Intuitive behavior is, at basis, expressive behavior, a "feeling toward" some motor-affective consummation on the basis of a tacitly anticipated equilibration (or harmonization) of bodily tensions. Such intuition, as Joseph Royce states, is invariably an esthetic process which is directed, as all esthetic processes are, toward the fullest expression of some activity-- ranging from the directly motor to the cognitive--which can be experienced as a sense of positive emotional "closure."[8]

In his work on self-actualization, Abraham Maslow refers to such moments of extreme emotional consummation as "peak experiences," which he defines rather generally as "a tremendous intensification of _any_ of the experiences in which there is a loss of self or transcendence of it, e.g., in problem centering, intense concentration, as described by Benedict [in her unpublished lectures on Synergy in Society], intense sensuous experience, self-forgetful and intense enjoyment of music or art."[9]

Such peak experiences, according to Maslow, are highly analogous to the experiences described by many mystics, but they are not in any sense "supernatural." Quite the contrary, they are natural experiences "well within the jurisdiction of science."[10]

Such experiences occur spontaneously. As Maslow notes: "We cannot command the peak-experience. It happens _to_ us."[11] "Peaks are not planned or brought about by design; they happen. We are [the words of D. M. Levy] "surprised by joy."[12]

Such experiences may occur in significantly different degrees of intensity, ranging from apocalyptic orgasms to mild esthetic highs,[13] and they occur with significantly different frequencies in different individuals.[14]

In his later years, Maslow became increasingly interested in the phenomenon of the peak-experience and he even began to speculate about differences in the reports of "peaking" among the self-actualizing people he was studying. As he notes in the revised edition (1970) of his <u>Motivation and Personality,</u>

"I have learned through the years since this study was first begun in 1935... to lay far greater stress than I had at first on the differences between 'peakers' and 'nonpeakers.' Most likely this is a difference of degree or amount, but it is a very important difference. Some of its consequences are set forth in considerable detail in an earlier article which appeared in the <u>Journal of Transpersonal Psychology.</u> If I had to sum it up very briefly, I would say that the nonpeaking self-actualizers seem so far to tend to be practical, effective people, mesomorphs living in the world and doing very well in it. Peakers also seem to live in the realm of Being; of poetry, esthetics; symbols; transcendence; 'religion' of the mystical, personal, noninstitutional sort; and of end-experiences. My prediction is that this will turn out to be one of the crucial characterological 'class differences,' crucial especially for social life because it looks as though the 'merely healthy' nonpeaking self-actualizers seem likely to be the social world improvers, the politicians, the workers in society, the reformers, the crusaders, whereas the transcending peakers are more apt to write the poetry, music, the philosophies, and the religions" (Maslow. <u>Motivation and Personality</u>, Revised Edition, p. 165)

Examples of peak experiences abound in the great works of literature, in religion, in philosophy and in psychology, but one fact seems evident: the essential characteristic of a peak-experience is not its particular content but rather its distinctive <u>quality as an experience</u>. It is, to borrow D. T. Suzuki's well-known definition of <u>satori</u>, "just like ordinary experience, except about two inches off the ground!"[15] Life goes on as usual, but it is suddenly <u>experienced</u> differently.

The object or event which elicits the experience can be virtually anything. Thus, for the great Irish poet William Butler Yeats, it occurred in middle age in a London coffee shop:

"My fiftieth year had come and gone,
I sat, a solitary man,
In a crowded London shop,
An open book and empty cup
On the marble table-top.

While on the shop and street I gazed
My body of a sudden blazed;
In twenty minutes more or less
It seemed, so great my happiness,
That I was blessed and could bless."[16]

For Pascal it was the presence of God:

"The year of grace 1654.
Monday the 23rd of November, St. Clement's day....
From about half past ten in the evening
Until half past twelve, midnight
FIRE
God of Abraham. God of Isaac. God of Jacob
not of the philosophers and the wise.
Certainty, joy, certainty, feeling, joy, peace."[17]

For William James it was a sense of total illumination:

"The very heavens seemed to open and pour down rays of light and glory. Not for a moment only, but all day and night, floods of light and glory seemed to pour through my soul, and oh, how I was changed, and everything became new. My horses and hogs and everybody seemed changed."[18]

For philosopher Richard Bucke, this sort of experience occurred while standing on a porch in the middle of the night looking at the stars:

"All at once, without warning of any kind, I found myself wrapped in a flame-colored cloud. For an instant I thought of fire, an immense conflagration somewhere close by in that great city; the next, I knew that the fire was within myself. Directly afterward there came upon me a sense of exultation, of immense joyousness accompanied or immediately followed by an intellectual illumination impossible to describe. Among other things, I did not merely come to believe, but I found that the universe is not composed of dead matter, but is, on the contrary, a living Presence; I became conscious in myself of eternal life. It was not a conviction that I would have eternal life, but a consciousness that I possessed eternal life then; I saw that all men are immortal; that the cosmic order is such that without any pre-adventure all things work together for the good of each and all; that the foundation principle of the world, of all the worlds, is what we call love, and that the happiness of each and all is in the long run absolutely certain. The vision lasted a few seconds and was gone; but the memory of it and the sense of the reality of what it taught has remained during the quarter of a century which has since elapsed."[19]

For still another anonymous witness the illumination occurred in a grimy railroad station:

"Suddenly, I was aware of some mysterious current of force, subtle, yet of unimagined potency, which seemed to sweep through that small drab waiting-room. A kind of glory descended upon the gathered company--or so it seemed to me. I looked at the faces of those around me and they seemed to be suffused with an inner radiance. I experienced in that moment a sense of profoundest kinship with each and every person there. I loved them all!--with a kind of love I had never felt before. It was an all-embracing emotion, which bound us together indissolubly in a deep unity of being. I lost all sense of personal identity then. These people were no longer strangers to me. I knew them all. We were no longer separate individuals, each enclosed in his own private world, divided by all the barriers of social convention and personal exclusiveness. We were one with each other and with the Life which we all lived in common."[20]

For Albert Camus, on still another occasion, it was elicited by the landscape near Florence:

"Millions of eyes have looked at this landscape [at Fiesole], and for me it is like the first smile of the world. It takes me out of myself, in the deepest meaning of the expression. It assures me that nothing matters except my love, and that even this love has no value for me unless it remains innocent and free. It denies me a personality and deprives my suffering of its echo. The world is beautiful, and this is everything. The great truth which impatiently teaches me that neither the mind nor the heart has any importance. And that the stone warmed by the sun or the cypress swelling against the empty sky set a boundary to the only world in which 'to be right' has any meaning; nature without men. This world reduces me to nothing. It carries me to the very end. Without anger, it denies that I exist. And, agreeing with my defeat, I move toward a wisdom where everything has been already conquered--except that tears come into my eyes, and this great sob of poetry makes me forget the truth of the world."[21]

For playwright John Van Druten it was a breakfast in a Beverly Hills drugstore:

"...an experience occurred to me about three years ago, and I tried the same morning to record it in a diary, hastily, with no attempt at good writing but in a form that was hardly more than a series of rough notes by which I would be able to recall it as it had seemed to me at the time of its happening, uncolored by any possible later memories of it as a memory. Here are the notes, just as I wrote them then:

"It was in a drugstore in Beverly Hills, when I had just sat down to breakfast at the counter. Beside me sat a very large and very healthy man in work-clothes--a man in his forties, I would say--eating a very large and healthy breakfast of fried eggs, hotcakes, and potatoes. They looked good: <u>he</u> looked good, exuding an unconscious physical strength and well-being. The food looked good in the way that painted food in advertisements looks good.

Suddenly I saw everything around me like that. A colored woman brought in a tray of raw hamburgers--round, pinky-gold pats--that looked inordinately appetizing. I looked at all the food, and it all had the same quality. The waitress, small and dumpy, was smiling and friendly; having served her customers, she looked around and asked, 'Well, is everyone happy here?' Everyone seemed to be. Each person, like the food, seemed <u>right</u> and meaningful. The fat, high-capped chef, tying on an apron that compressed him with its string like a bundle of laundry: all the customers: there was not one ugly person there. I don't mean that they were all good-looking--but that there was not one bad, or even stupid or irritating face among them. The whole scene looked as though it had been painted by a great and loving painter, who had given it its own and timeless values. From there on, my notes go into an attempt to analyze the meaning of the experience which lasted, I would guess, about fifteen minutes in all."[22]

The peak experience is more than a sense of extreme emotional closure, however. It is a moment of emotional consummation, but it is also a release from the confines of conventional selfhood. It is, in a sense, the total happiness that grows out of total sanity, and, conversely, the total sanity that grows out of total happiness.

In peaking, the self-actualizing person experiences a very real sense of fusion with his situation, of participating in Being; in a sense, he transcends the traditional boundaries of the ego altogether. The result is an intense experience of union, of "oneness"--what Freud sometimes called the "oceanic feeling."[23] Such a state is neither a <u>being</u> nor a <u>doing</u> in the usual sense of these terms but, rather, a total sense of being deeply "involved" with <u>whatever</u> one is doing. Indeed, in the peak experience <u>becoming</u> becomes <u>being</u>.

In the original Aristotelian sense, the organism (to quote philosopher John Herman Randall) "takes sensing as the vehicle of meaning, as the setting in operation of the 'sensible forms' of things; and it views that process of 'actualization' as the joint cooperation of powers, involving powers of both the sensing organism to sense, and of the environment to be sensed."[24]

Such experience corresponds closely to what John Dewey frequently referred to as the "transactio" relationship between the organism and its environment "It is," to quote Alan Watts, "like, not watching, but being a coiling arabesque of smoke patterns in the air, or of ink dropped in water, or of a dancing snake which seems to move from every part of its body at once."[25] It is, like Camus' description of night at the top of the Vaucluse, a sort of "lucid ecstasy" in which "the milky way comes down through the clusters of lights in the valley. Everything is mixed up. There are villages in the sky and constellations in the mountainside." In the religious metaphors employed by Ortega, the individual "ceases, in effect, to be <u>objectum</u> and becomes <u>injectum</u>. God filters into the soul and merges with it or, inversely, the soul dilutes into God and no longer feels that He is a different being from itself. This is the unio (union) to which the mystic aspires."[27]

In a sense, then, the peak-experience is an almost total love-relationship in which the experienced difference between self and non-self virtually disappears and in which conventional awareness becomes almost entirely intuitive. Consciousness becomes total, holistic, Gestalt. It apprehends the world synthetically, without the usual artificial distinctions and divisions. Indeed, the traditional analytic differences within experience no longer apply. Awareness becomes nonlinear, nonrelational--in a conventional sense "disoriented." As Fritz Perl's and his associates note:

"In such a whole-of-parts the figure provides its own boundary. Therefore there are no ego-functions; no boundaries are chosen, there are no identifications and alienations, and no further deliberateness. The experience is entirely intrinsic; one is in no way acting on it. The relaxation of deliberateness and the vanishing of boundaries is the reason for the extra brightness and vigor--e.g., the 'flash of insight' or the 'shock of recognition'--for the energy that went into withholding oneself or aggressively putting connections into the environment is now suddenly added to the final spontaneous experience."[28]

In the pre-potency of the moment, even time and space relationships dissolve. The experience becomes "eternal" and "infinite," not because it is in any real sense "timeless" or "spaceless" but because the very notions of conventional time and space become profoundly irrelevant. The moment has become "non-temporal," "non-spatial." Again, and as Maslow states:

"In all the common peak-experiences which I have studied, there is a very characteristic disorientation in time and space. It would be accurate to say that in these moments the person is outside of time and space subjectively. In the creative furor, the poet or artist becomes oblivious of his surroundings, and of the passage of time. It is impossible for him when he wakes up to judge how much time has passed. Frequently he has to shake his head as if emerging from a daze to rediscover where he is."[29]

In peak-experience, the individual is most here-now, most free of the past and of the future in various senses, most "all there" in the experience. For instance, he can now listen better than at other times. Since he is least habitual and least expectant, he can fully listen without contamination by dragging in expectations (which can't be identically like the present one), or hopes or apprehensions based on planning for the future (which means taking the present only as means to the future rather than as end in itself). Since also he is beyond desire, he needn't rubricize in terms of fear, hate or wish. Nor does he have to compare what is here with what is not here in order to evaluate it.[31]

"... being in a state of Being needs no future, because it is already there. Becoming ceases for the moment and its promissory notes are cashed in, in the form of the ultimate rewards, i.e., the peak-experience in which time disappears and hopes are fulfilled."[32]

Such observations are reminiscent of the great Christian mystic Meister Eckhart:

"Time is what keeps the light from reaching us. There is no greater obstacle to God than time. And not only time but temporalities, not only temporal things but temporal affections; not only temporal affections but the very taint and smell of time."[33]

In the peak-experience, then, the individual loses himself in the larger "Self" of his situation. He becomes part of that "ground of Being" which Paul Tillich calls "God." Again to quote Eckhart:

"As long as I am this or that, or have this or that, I am not all things and I have not all things. Become pure till you neither are nor have either this or that; then you are omnipresent and, being neither this nor that, are all things."[34]

As esthetician Bernard Berenson once observed, "A complete life may be one ending in so full an identification with the not-self that there is no self left to die." [34]
In the peak-experience, consciousness ceases to be <u>self</u>-consciousness, and human becoming emerges into a direct and awe-inspiring relationship with encompassing being. As Maslow notes,

"<u>The emotional reaction in the peak-experience has a special flavor of wonder, of awe, of reverence, of humility and surrender before the experience as before something great.</u> This sometimes has a touch of fear (although pleasant fear) of being overwhelmed. My subjects report this in such phrases as 'This is too much for me.' 'It is more than I can bear.' 'It is too wonderful.' The experience may have a certain poignancy and piercing quality which may bring either tears or laughter or both, and which may be paradoxically akin to pain, although this is a desirable pain which is often described as 'sweet'. This may go so far as to involve thoughts of death in a peculiar way."[35]

"Crossing a bare common," says Emerson, "in snow puddles, at twilight, under a clouded sky, without having in my thoughts any occurrence of special good fortune. I have enjoyed a perfect exhilaration. I am glad to the brink of fear."[36] It is, to quote William Blake,

"To see a World in a Grain of Sand
And a Heaven in a Wild flower,
Hold Infinity in the palm of your hand
And Eternity in an hour."[37]

Peak experiences are related to what Maslow has popularized as "Being-cognition," but they are the sort of Being-cognition in which "total" attention melds into total absorption.[38] Such an experience is "as if the percept had become for the moment the whole of Being."[39] As in a heightened sort of Being-cognition "the experience or the object tends to be seen as a whole, as a complete unit, detached from relations, from possible usefulness, from expediency, and from purpose. It is seen as if it were all there was in the universe, as if it were all of Being, synonymous with the universe."[40]

Peak experiences serve as the highest type of pleasure--the maximum sort of reward or reinforcement for those who are capable of experiencing them. Those who undergo peak experiences feel "lucky, fortunate, graced."[41] They experience themselves as "more integrated (unified, whole, all-of-a-piece), than at other times,"[42] and this sense of unity is inevitably experienced as a sense of total well-being which transcends normal feelings of pleasure or happiness altogether. Indeed, and as Maslow notes, the experience is so total that it "is felt as a self-validating, self-justifying moment which carries its own intrinsic value with it. That is to say it is an end in itself, which we may call an end-experience rather than a means-experience."[43]

"[It] is intrinsically valid; the experience is perfect, complete and needs nothing else. It is sufficient to itself. It is felt as being intrinsically necessary and inevitable. It is just as good as it <u>should</u> be. It is reacted to with awe, wonder, amazement, humility and even reverence, exaltation and piety. The word <u>sacred</u> is occasionally used to describe the person's reaction to it. It is delightful and 'amusing' in a Being sense."[44]

For the self-actualizer such moments are almost sacramental, reaffirming their faith in life as it is understood to be, and verifying their dedication to spontaneous and creative experience. The self-actualizing person who undergoes a peak experience feels renewed.

As he gets to be more purely and singly himself he is more able to fuse with the world, with what was formerly not-self, e.g., the lovers come closer to forming a unit rather than two people, the I-Thou becomes more possible, the creator becomes one with his work being created, the mother feels one with her child, the appreciator becomes the music (and it becomes <u>him</u>) or the painting, or the dance, the astronomer is "out there" with the stars (rather than a separateness peering through an abyss at another separateness through a telescopic-keyhole).[45]

The person in peak-experiences feels himself, more than at other times, to be the responsible, active, creating center of his activities and of his perceptions. He feels more like a prime mover, more self-determined (rather than caused, determined, helpless, dependent, passive, weak, bossed). He feels himself to be his own boss, fully responsible, fully volitional, with more "free will" than at other times, master of his fate.[46]

For the non-actualizer, it is not only a profoundly rewarding experience but even a therapeutic one. As Maslow states:

"Peak-experiences may and do have some therapeutic effects in the strict sense of removing symptoms. I have at least two reports--one from a psychologist, one from an anthropologist--of mystic or oceanic experiences so profound as to remove certain neurotic symptoms forever after. Such conversion experiences are of course plentifully recorded in human history but so far as I know have never received the attention of psychologists or psychiatrists."[47]

Some of the therapeutic characteristics of the peak-experience stem from the fact that "one aspect of the peak-experience is a complete, though momentary, loss of fear, anxiety, inhibition, defense and control, a giving up of renunciation, delay and restraint."[48]

The fear of disintegration and dissolution, the fear of being overwhelmed by the "instincts," the fear of death and of insanity, the fear of giving in to unbridled pleasure and emotion, all tend to disappear or go into abeyance for the time being. This too implies a greater openness of perception since fear distorts.[49]

On the other hand, this is only part of the picture, for, in a more basic sense, peak-experiences also have far more general consequences. Maslow lists some of these as follows:

"They can change the person's view of himself in a healthy direction. They can change his view of other people and his relations to them in many ways.
They can change more or less permanently his view of the world, or of aspects or parts of it.
They can release him for greater creativity, spontaneity, expressiveness, idiosyncrasy."[50]

But peak-experiences also have a cognitive-conative function. They serve as dynamic motivating insights into a different kind of reality than that ordinarily experienced, becoming, to use a phrase of Edgar Z.

Friedenberg, "moments of truth so penetrating and luminous that the rest of life is brightened by them."[51]

For the non-actualizer such moments are profoundly affecting because they provide a "phenomenological proof" that a different and better way of living really exists. They become, in effect, those irrevocable moments of sanity--those fleeting moments in which one has a subjective sense of objective awareness--which become capable of throwing a person's normal processes of experience into radical doubt. Indeed, in one sense, it is precisely the sort of emotional perspective which grows out of these moments in which the individual transcends conventional thinking and feeling that demonstrate that there is a realm of reality which goes beyond normal experience.

Frequently, they become the basis for a totally new sense of value, becoming, in effect, a sort of hallmark emotional criterion by which it becomes possible to reexamine and reevaluate the course of conventional awareness. In becoming momentarily sane, the individual gains a healing insight into his own habitual "non-sanity." Beyond these things, however, many of these moments remain vivid, and. begin to function as values as well as mere experiences, "moments out of time." In a sense, he predicted his own end as one possible scenario in his writings, and his very death was a partial confirmation of his vision. Certainly his death does not disqualify his actions, because life is inherently tragic, and everyone's life--self-actualizing or otherwise--ends in death. This is one of the reasons that censors frequently make a grave error in assuming that virtually any kind of immorality can be sanctioned so long as the villain is killed in the end. *Everyone* is killed in the end, and even children recognize that an exciting life that leads to death with a bang is probably a better choice than an innocuous existence that leads to death as a whimper.[52]

In one of his writings Gide describes a moment of total joy which he once experienced in Africa, and he relates how he spent the rest of his life seeking repetition of this moment.[53]

In a sense, this exemplifies the most important function of the peak-experience. As Maslow states, "The person is more apt to feel that life in general is worthwhile, even if it is usually drab, pedestrian, painful or ungratifying, since beauty, excitement, honesty, play, goodness, truth and meaningfulness have been demonstrated to him to exist."[54] "He remembers the experience as a very important and desirable happening and seeks to repeat it."[55]

In its way, then, the peak-experience is more than a moment of ecstasy; it is also experienced as a dynamic insight that is fully capable of functioning as a motive, a "qualitative-pervasive," which operates on a more or less intuitive basis as both a moment to be remembered and, hopefully, a moment to be relived. In this sense, peak experiences are heuristic and central to the entire process of psychological synergy which lies at the heart of the self-actualized.

Emotionally, peak-experiences constitute the highest form of self-gratification, and they provide the emotional basis for perceptual objectivity. Cognitively, they serve as a quasi-intuitive view into the highest and most fully satisfying sort of human experience. Volitionally, they provide the ultimate goal for all ongoing behavior. Normatively, they provide the basis for the evaluation--in a sense, for the "transvaluation"--of all normal experience.

Endnotes for Chapter 16

1. Gilbert Ryle, <u>The Concept of Mind</u> (New York Barnes and Noble, 1949), p. 58.
2. Michael Polanyi, <u>Personal Knowledge: Towards a Post-Critical Philosophy</u> (Chicago: University of Chicago Press, 1958),
3. Daisetz T. Suzuki, in D. T. Suzuki, Erich Fromm and Richard de Martino, <u>Zen Buddhism and Psychoanalysis</u> (New York: Grove Press, Inc., 1960), pp. 48-49.
4. Albert Camus, <u>The Myth of Sisyphus and Other Essays</u> (New York Alfred A. Knopf--Vintage, 1960), p. 143.
5. Bernard Berenson, <u>Sketch for a Self-Portrait</u> (Bloomington, Indiana Indiana University Press, 1949), p. 18.
6. <u>Ibid</u>., p. 21.
7. Alan W. Watts, <u>The Way of Zen</u> (New York New American Library--Mentor, 1957), p. 33.
8. Joseph Royce. <u>The Encapsulated Man</u> New York Van Nostrand--Insight, 1964, pp. 15-16.
9. Abraham H. Maslow, <u>Motivation and Personality</u>. Second Edition. (New York Harper and Row Publishers, 1970), P. 165.
10. p. 164.
11. Abraham H. Maslow, <u>Toward a Psychology of Being </u>(New York Van Nostrand Company, 1962), p. 82.
12. <u>Ibid</u>., p. 106.

13. Maslow, <u>Motivation and Personality</u> Second Edition. (New York Harper and Row Publishers, 1970), p. 164.

14. Maslow, <u>Motivation and Personality</u> Revised Edition, p. 165).

15. Daisetz T. Suzuki, quoted in Alan W. Watts, <u>The Way of Zen</u> pp. 33-34.

16. William Butler Yeats, <u>Poems</u> (New York Macmillan, 1956), p. 135.

17. Blaise Pascal, quoted in Alan W. Watts, <u>This is It and Other Essays</u> (New York Collier Books, 1967), p. 19.

18. William James, quoted in Watts, <u>This is It</u> p. 20,

19. Richard Maurice Bucke, <u>Cosmic Consciousness</u> quoted in William James, <u>Varieties of Religious Experience</u> (New York: New American Library--Mentor, 1958), pp. 306-307.

20. Raynor G. Johnson, <u>Watcher on the Hill</u> (New York Harper, 1959), pp. 84-85.

21. Albert Camus, <u>Notebooks: 1935-1942</u> (New York Random House--Modem Library, 1965), p. 56.

22. John Van Druten, in Christopher Isherwood (ed.), <u>Vedarita for Modem Man</u> (New . York: Collier Books),pp. 411-412.

23. Abrahan H. Maslow, <u>Motivation and Personality</u> (New York Harper and Row Publishers. 1954), pp 215-216.

24. John Herman Randall, Jr., <u>Aristotle</u> (New York Columbia University Press, 1960), p 87

25. Watts, <u>This is It</u> pp. 138-139.

26. A Camus, <u>Notebooks: 1942-1951</u> (New York: Harcourt Brace Jovanovich, 1965). p. 199.

27. Jose Ortega y Gasset, <u>On Love: Aspects of a Single Theme</u> Translated by Toby Talbot. (New York: Meridian Books, Inc., 1960), p. 63.

28. Frederick Perls, Ralph F. Hefferline and Paul Goodman, <u>Gestalt Therapy: Excitement and Growth in the Human Personality</u> (New York Dell Publishing--Delta, 1951), p. 417.

29. Abraham H. Maslow, <u>Toward a Psychology of Being</u> (New York D. Van Nostrand Company, Inc., 1962), pp. 75-76.

30. <u>Ibid</u>., pp. 79-80.

31. <u>Ibid</u>., p. 102.

32. Ibid., p. 200.

33. Meister Eckhart, quoted in Aldous Huxley, The Perennial Philosophy (New York Harper and Brothers Publishers, 1945), p. 189.

34. Meister Eckhart, quoted in Huxley, The Perennial Philosophy p. 107.

35. Maslow, Toward a Psychology of Being p. 82.

36. Ralph Waldo Emerson, quoted in William James, Essays on Faith and Morals (New York: The World Publishing Company, 1962), p. 279.

37. William Blake, "Auguries of Innocence," quoted in I. A. Richards, Coleridge on Imagination (New York Norton, 1950), p. 66.

38. Maslow, Toward a Psychology of Being p. 70.

39. Ibid., p. 70.

40. Ibid.

41. Ibid., p. 106.

42. Ibid., p. 98.

43. Ibid., p.74.

44. Ibid., p.76

45. Ibid., p. 99.

46. Ibid., p. 100.

47. Ibid., p. 95.

48. Ibid., p. 89.

49. Ibid.

50. Ibid., p. 95.

51. Edgar Z. Friedenberg, The Dignity of Youth and Other Atavisms (Boston: Beacon Press, 1965), p. 34.

52. Erich Fromm, Man for Himself (New York: Holt, Rinehart and Winston 1947). p. 230.

53. Eliseo Vivas, The Moral Life and the Ethical Life (Chicago: Henry Regnery Co., 1963), p. 182.

54. Maslow, Toward a New Psychology of Being p. 95.

55. Ibid.

References for Chapters 1-15

Berelson, Bernard <u>Human Behavior.</u>

Brown, Norman <u>Life Against Death</u>.

Bruner, Jerome 1963 <u>On Knowing</u>. Cambridge: Harvard University Press.

Camus, Albert 1965a <u>Notebooks: 1935-1942.</u> New York: Random House.

_____ 1965b <u>Notebooks: 1942-1951.</u> New York: Harcourt Brace Jovanovich.

Croce, Benedetto

Erickson, Erik 1994 <u>Identity: Youth and Crisis.</u> W. W. Norton and Company.

Fromm, Erich 1947 <u>Man for Himself.</u> New York: Holt, Rinehart and Winston.

_____ 1956 <u>The Sane Society.</u>

_____ 1962 <u>Beyond the Chains of Illusion.</u>

Hospers, John 1953 <u>An Introduction to Philosophical Analysis.</u> New Jersey: Prentice Hall

_____ 1961 <u>Human Conduct.</u>

James, William 1956 <u>The Will to Believe.</u> New York: Dover Publishing, Inc.

Kaplan, Abraham 1963 <u>The New World of Philosophy.</u>

Keene, S. C. 1952 <u>Introduction to Mathematics.</u>

Langer, Susanne 1957 <u>Philosophy in a New Key.</u>

London, Perry <u>The Modes and Morals of Psychotherapy.</u>

Maier, Norman 1960 "Experimentally Induced Abnormal Behavior," in Morris Haimowitz and Natalie Haimowitz, (eds.), <u>Human Development.</u> New York: Thomas Crowell.

_____ 1961 <u>Frustration.</u> Ann Arbor, Michigan: University of Michigan Press.

Mannheim, Karl 1936 <u>An ideology and Utopia.</u> Orlando, Florida: Harcourt, Inc.

Maslow, Abraham 1954 <u>Motivation and Personality.</u> 2nd ed. 1970. New York: Harper and Row Publishers.

_____ 1962 <u>Toward a Psychology of Being.</u> New York: Van Nostrand Co.

_____ 1971 <u>New Knowledge in Human Values.</u>

May, Rollo <u>Existence.</u>

Mc Luhan, Marshall <u>The Medium is the Message.</u>

Miller, Henry 1963 <u>Correspondence with Lawrence Durrell.</u> Time Magazine, March 1.

Mumford, Lewis 1951 <u>The Conduct of Life.</u> New York: Harcourt, Brace and Company.

Ortega y Gasset, Jose 1960 <u>On Love.</u> New York: Meridian Books, Inc.

Perry, Ralph 1954 <u>Realms of Value.</u>

Polanyi, Michael 1958 <u>Personal Knowledge.</u> Chicago: University of Chicago Press.

_____ 1960 <u>The Study of Man.</u>

Royce, Joseph 1964 <u>The Encapsulated Man.</u> New York: Van Nostrand Co.

Rugg, Harold 1963 <u>Imagination.</u>

Russell, E. S. 1946 <u>The Directiveness of Organic Activities.</u> Cambridge, England: Cambridge University Press.

Ryle, Gilbert 1949 <u>The Concept of Mind.</u> New York: Barnes and Noble.

Shaw, George <u>Man and Superman.</u>

Smith, T. V. and Debbins, William 1948 <u>Constructive Ethics.</u> Prentice Hall.

Sorokin, Pitirim <u>The Ways and Power of Love.</u>

Suzuki, D. T. 1956 <u>Zen Buddhism.</u> New York: Doubleday and Co., Inc.

Vivas, Eliseo 1963 <u>The Moral Life and the Ethical Life.</u> Chicago: Henry Regnery Co.

Watts, Alan 1957 <u>The Way of Zen.</u> New York: New American Library.

Watts, Alan 1958 <u>Nature, Man and Woman.</u> New York: New American Library.

_____ 1961 <u>Psychotherapy East and West.</u> New York: New American Library.

Wellman, Henry.

Wiener, Norbert <u>The Human Use of Human Beings.</u>

Dr. William F. O'Neill is a professor Emeritus in the School of Education at the University of Southern California in the Department of Policy, Planning and Administration. He received his PhD in Education from USC. He also did graduate work at the University of Vienna (Austria), UCLA, and CSULB.

Dr. O'Neill taught globally at numerous universities in the areas of international education, educational policy studies, and the social and philosophical foundations of education.

He has written several books in and around the area of educational philosophy including: <u>Selected Educational Heresies</u> (1969), <u>Readin, Ritin and Rafferty</u> (1969), <u>With Charity Toward None: An Analysis of Ayn Rand's Philosophy</u> (1970), and <u>Educational Ideologies: Social Philosophies and Education</u>. He has also written over 75 academic journal articles for a variety of different publications in the fields of philosophy, psychology and education.

Dr O'Neill has had extensive administrative experience in higher education, serving as Chairman of the Department of Social and Philosophical Foundations of Education at USC and also directing several overseas programs dealing with international education. He was director of the Educational Policy Studies Program at the USC Washington Education Center in Washington, D.C. for many years. Additionally, he has worked as a consultant for the United States government as well as for a variety of school districts, colleges, and universities.

Dr O'Neill is Past-President of the American Educational Studies Association, the major professional organization focusing on the social and philosophical foundations of education. During his career he was actively engaged in both conducting and supervising research in international education, educational administration, and educational philosophy.

Upon retiring from USC he began working on two additional books, one dealing with Eastern philosophies and education and the other concerned with the educational implications of Abraham Maslow's theory of self-actualization.

George Demos PhD served 30 years as Professor of Counseling Psychology at California State University Long Beach. Dr. Demos practiced as a clinical psychologist for 40 years. He has served the past five years as President of the Post Traumatic Stress Disorder (PTSD) project, helping returning veterans. He also served 30 years in the military active duty and reserve army (retired Colonel).

CPSIA information can be obtained at www.ICGtesting.com
Printed in the USA
BVOW040346201112

305941BV00002B/3/P